MW01295687

"After a tragedy you often
account of a heart-wrenchi
she encounters Jesus in her grief. Kate testifies
does come into our darkest moments to reveal Himself as comforter,
refuge, companion and guide. If you are encountering grief, or if you
know someone in grief, I heartily recommend this book to you to
learn the ways of God in our suffering."

RUTH GRAHAM
Author & speaker, Ruth Graham Ministries

"Few people are able to tell their story in a way that connects the pain
of life with the purposes and peace of heaven. Kate Kelty does just
that. This book will make you weep. It will drive you to your knees
in prayer. It will lift your spirit to heaven and it will bless your soul."

CARMEN FOWLER LABERGE
President of the Presbyterian Lay Committee

"This valuable book is a living story of Kate Kelty's documented
journey: from deep despair to unexplainable peace; from laborious
coping to needed resolution; from mere knowledge to Godly
revelations; from painful suppression to reluctant admission of
explainable anger and disappointment; from carrying weighty
burdens to giving them away; from false perceptions to absolute
truths and freedom from a distorted view of a Heavenly Father to
the Jesus of her grief."

STEPHEN JOHNSON
LCSW/Counselor, Stephen Johnson and Associates,
Lexington, Kentucky

"Being an OB/GYN in practice for 20 years, I have shared this
journey of loss with women more often than I like. Additionally,
I lost my own son, David, before his birth. The pain and grief that
Kate walks us through is genuine and the reminders are daily. Her
journey with Christ brings hope and reassurance that Jesus is there
for our grief, our present and our future. The purpose for the child
becomes evident as Kate struggles and resolves her suffering. Peace at

last. I welcome this book as an aid to help future young couples learn to turn their despair into peaceful resolution through His grace."

**CATHY SLUSHER**
M.D., Harrisonburg OB/GYN Associates
Medical Director of Obstetrics for Sentara RMH,
Harrisonburg, Virginia

"No matter the source of your personal walk through grief, this book will inspire hope in your heart and faith in a living, loving God. Kate's eloquent words will sweep you into her real life encounters and allow you to see for yourself the tenderness of Jesus in times of turmoil. We will all face grief in this life, but this story proves that true hope is possible in spite of it."

**JESSICA CRAWFORD**
Missionary & musician; Nashville, Tennessee

"During my darkest days, Kate was my greatest gift of grief. Losing a child is one of the most devastating journeys a parent can walk. For those that grieve and walk the dark road of loss, this raw and real story will leave you with hope."

**ALICIA BERRY**
Harrisonburg, Va

"On September 28, 2011, without any warning or detectable cause, our precious 6-month-old granddaughter, Aria Joy, passed away in her sleep. Never had we known such gut-wrenching grief and unquenchable pain. Watching our daughter and her family grieve was truly unbearable. Enter…The Jesus of My Grief. Kate Kelty has an extraordinary God-given gift for putting words on paper. THIS IS NOT JUST ANOTHER BOOK. This is a SACRED EXPERIENCE! I implore you friend, come partake and experience a supernatural encounter with the God who is greater than your grief. I can promise, you will receive a heavenly impartation of the "grace to grieve and the power to be made whole."

**BRYNN WADE**
Lexington, Kentucky

# THE JESUS OF MY GRIEF

### From Pain to Peace Through Visions of the Savior

## KATE KELTY

WESTBOW°
PRESS
A DIVISION OF THOMAS NELSON
& ZONDERVAN

Scriptures taken from the Holy Bible, New International Version®, NIV®. Copyright © 1973, 1978, 1984, 2011 by Biblica, Inc.™ Used by permission of Zondervan. All rights reserved worldwide. www.zondervan.com The "NIV" and "New International Version" are trademarks registered in the United States Patent and Trademark Office by Biblica, Inc.™ All rights reserved.

WestBow Press books may be ordered through booksellers or by contacting:

WestBow Press
A Division of Thomas Nelson & Zondervan
1663 Liberty Drive
Bloomington, IN 47403
www.westbowpress.com
1 (866) 928-1240

Because of the dynamic nature of the Internet, any web addresses or links contained in this book may have changed since publication and may no longer be valid. The views expressed in this work are solely those of the author and do not necessarily reflect the views of the publisher, and the publisher hereby disclaims any responsibility for them.

Any people depicted in stock imagery provided by Thinkstock are models, and such images are being used for illustrative purposes only. Certain stock imagery © Thinkstock.

ISBN: 978-1-4908-3729-1 (sc)
ISBN: 978-1-4908-3730-7 (hc)
ISBN: 978-1-4908-3728-4 (e)

Library of Congress Control Number: 2014909039

Printed in the United States of America.

WestBow Press rev. date: 06/24/2014

# For my husband...

*Thank you for being Jesus to me in the days when I couldn't see or feel Him. Thank you for forsaking your own needs time and time again to comfort and encourage me. For making our darkest days the brightest in love, you are my hero. You are tenderness, wisdom and patience to our children and I admire and am proud to be your wife. You were right, "There will be joy," and it's been you time and time again. Here's to our favorite word, our favorite color, our favorite everything, Anna.*

# For my children...

*Being your mama is my life's greatest joy.*
*To you I have but one word- Jesus.*

# For Anna...

*I wouldn't change a thing baby girl. Loving you and the revelations therein, have been the greatest privilege of my life. Keep watching...*

# CONTENTS

PART ONE

# GRIEF

# CHAPTER 1

# INTRODUCTION TO SORROW

*"Everything I had hoped for from the Lord is lost."*

*Lamentations 3:18 (NLT)*

One cold morning on the edge of spring during my junior year of college, I was driving to campus when I heard a voice, that is, *the still, small voice*, giving me directions. The whisper spoke to my mind, and I clearly discerned, "Drive straight." I looked to my right as I passed my destination in a trusting state of shock and wonder. Nothing like this had ever happened to me before. "Turn left." I continued driving as if I were going home, a route worn with familiarity, and yet I hadn't a clue. After several more directions, I found myself pulling through the large wrought iron gates of the Lexington Cemetery. I was overcome by confusion and also certain that this was exactly where I was supposed to be.

I parked my car and timidly, yet anxiously, got out and began walking. I wasn't exactly sure what I was looking for, but I felt in my heart that when I found it, I would know. Several minutes went by as I followed different paths through the cemetery, and then I saw it. I was standing at the top of a steep hill which led down into a small circular valley. The day was brisk and hazy, but the sun seemed to create a spotlight on the space below. I saw a tiny pond, a few large rocks, and a couple of dainty trees. Surrounding the spot were ancient oaks sitting as an audience, each with its own story to tell. It was a breathtaking, perfect sight, and it seemed so familiar, like I had seen it before hanging on a gallery wall. The contrast between this sea of graves and this hollow space of simple, natural beauty was striking. I stood there for a moment taking in the scene with one full breath before I took another step.

As I started down the hill, I remember wondering what Eve felt like as she strolled in the Garden of Eden almost entirely alone in the world. I felt like a part of history and somehow important as I made my journey to this place that had practically sent me an invitation. I nuzzled down next to a big rock looking at this humble little water hole, and I was instantly at home in the sunlight that warmed me. Every single flower caught my attention. The blooms were small and tiny and just an inch from the earth, but the changing seasons and the sun had called them out of hibernation and into a spring bursting with the promise of new life. I felt guilty that I was inspired in this haven embedded in a place where so many had suffered. But it was only a fleeting thought as I relaxed into the moment and took in the glory of having been led by God to such a threshold of His presence. I imagined a place just like it in eternity. It had been a dark year in my life, one marked with loneliness, the loss of a love once shared, and the agony of knowing it would never return. I picked up a few purple buds, mementos, placed them in my journal, and wrote…

> The difference between me and Eve as I walk in this garden is that I know my need for the Lord as I walk, run, crawl, hide, and am found in Him. I have the privilege in my weakness of knowing I need a Savior. But who is Jesus? My greatest desire is to know Him. I have felt Him and tasted Him so powerfully at times, and at other times He feels so distant. The valley I am in now makes me plead for Him to be my fullness, for loneliness is so terrible. As I sit here it almost feels like a dream or a room in my heart. I was made to be in glory with Him…this place whispers of that. One day…

4

The winter had frozen life out of me, and now the scattered warmth and rain of March told a new story. This secret place bursting with energy and glory was a beacon of hope for me in the midst of a season of loss. Everything in me resonated with this moment, and I felt so loved by God that He would allow me to experience His reminder of hope in such a supernatural way.

As I pulled out of the Lexington Cemetery that day, a seed of hope was planted in my heart, and I was sure that joy, purpose, and intimacy with God were new and permanent fixtures in my life. I never could have imagined that five years later on a similar March morning, I would be entering those wrought iron gates for the second time, like the unnumbered sufferers who had come before me.

## Five Years later

My husband parked the car, and I watched as he slowly walked inside the main building of the Lexington Cemetery. As I sat there alone, I suddenly remembered the day five years earlier when the Spirit had led me to this graveyard. I had felt so near to and so cared for by God. This was not such a day. The irony made me cold, and it would be several years until I could embrace these parallel encounters as a sovereign gift. I sat bracing myself for the suffering I knew was about to overtake me. The past month had passed in the same manner. Every day I braced myself until the inevitable wave of grief struck and wiped me out. Sometimes I was crying before I knew I was awake, and on other days I made it until noon. Chris opened the car door and reluctantly, but lovingly, placed a small brown box crowned with a death and cremation certificate into my hands. I was done.

On the evening of February 22, 2005, my husband and I received the most shocking and painful words we have ever heard.

I was nearly 37 weeks along in my first pregnancy, and two nurses were unable to find our daughter Anna's heartbeat. We waited for the doctor to arrive to relieve our unspeakable fears. As he said his, "I'm sorry," I began to scream as I stared at a monitor revealing my daughter's fully developed, yet motionless, heart.

Earlier that day, I had returned to my work as a counselor at the crisis pregnancy center after being terribly sick for two weeks. I had a burst of energy and excitement as I knew I had made it through the storm and was counting down the days until Anna girl's arrival. After work, I raced in the door to put all the pink clothes I had collected after my last baby shower into the washer. I couldn't wait to pull them out of the dryer, the smell of readiness, and to fold them neatly into her dresser. It was the last thing to cross off our "to do" list for Anna.

Her nursery was perfect. I had labored over every detail for months and had even painted her room twice to make sure it was the perfect shade of yellow. Chris and I had carefully chosen three scriptures which I painted to hang in her room. It felt like my own little sanctuary. It was so easy for me to meet with Jesus as I rocked, prayed, and sang to her. At Chris's instruction, the door to her room had been closed for two weeks to keep out my germs. I had missed our haven and my special moments with Anna so much.

It was about 10:00 o'clock at night when I allowed myself to realize I hadn't been feeling Anna move. We rushed to the hospital. In retrospect, I think my mind was unable to grasp what my heart already feared. As the life-shattering proclamation sank into my mind and heart, I cried out to Jesus. The doctor, who was also a believer, said, "Let me check again" with a rush of faith and desperation. He put the ultrasound probe back on my bulging belly which boasted of life. There was a moment when everyone in the room who knew the Jesus of the resurrection, the

Jesus who had brought a little girl back from the dead, believed that God could do the same miraculous wonder for us. Yet, once again, I stared at my motionless child and cried out as only a grieving mother can, as I held onto my husband and searched his eyes for a solution. I felt abandoned by God.

Three days later, Anna Rose Katherine Kelty was delivered into my arms, having already been delivered into the arms of God. We were the proud parents of all five pounds and five ounces of her fragile body. Strangely, supernaturally, the smile could not be wiped from her daddy's face. She was twenty inches long and had a head full of brown hair. Her tiny little mouth was a rosebud and her little nose, the sweetest button I've ever seen. Anna was exquisite.

For eleven hours Chris and I held her, prayed with her, sang to her, lay with her, smothered her with kisses, changed her, studied her, and enveloped her. Friend after friend entered our room and kissed her face and cried with us as they said hello and good-bye to our baby girl. Our parents and siblings wept for their pain and ours. The unthinkable had occurred. In the moments when I wasn't holding her, Chris cradled her, and I felt my heart go limp. I had never met a man like him who had been so joyous in anticipation of a baby. As my body had grown day after day, his heart had grown as well. Indeed, he had a pregnant heart. The only thing that deepened my agony was bearing witness to his.

Late that evening a precious nurse, Alice, who had so tenderly cared for us and our daughter, came to take Anna. It is the moment every expecting parent dreads, and it was happening to us. I had to relinquish my long anticipated and prayed-for baby to the grave, and I was completely unprepared and unwilling to endure this tragedy. Good-bye to nursing, good-bye to first smiles, cooing, and giggles. Good-bye to braids and kissing boo-boos. Good-bye to prom dresses and wedding dresses. Good-bye to daddy's little girl. Good-bye to a lifetime of anticipated everythings.

On February 22, 2005, my daughter died within me, and I died as well.

Many years have passed since that devastating day. For just over three years, I fought with a God I thought I knew and trusted. While pregnant with Anna, I had come to a place in my spiritual journey where I felt excited to be able to share His convincing and measureless love with the women in crisis I was counseling. I had marveled at and praised a God who could transform a woman's reluctant heart to love for a previously unwanted child. Now I growled at this same God for stealing from me. I had worked passionately to save babies, only now to lose my own. The pain and unfairness tortured me. The meaning of grace had escaped me.

My God of love had become a God of pain, the culprit of my senseless tragedy. Half of my soul was convinced of my need for God and begged for His comfort and love; the other half waged war against this Lord of stillbirth. A false and frightening god was being formed from the self-pitying perceptions of my tragedy and the lies of the enemy. Through three and a half years of battle, bargaining, panic, fear, loneliness, strongholds, rage, and too many tears to count, I beheld the beautiful and powerful face of God. I now know Him to be the Savior of the sad, the comforter of the weak, the giver of good, the supernatural restorer, the sovereign I AM, and the one true constant.

It happened slowly, one lie abolished, one truth absorbed at a time. I experienced what I can only describe as supernatural encounters with Jesus, visions of and with the Savior. Each encounter, a new brush stroke on a dark canvas to paint the real and true God I was seeking to know. Truthfully, I was also seeking to catch God red-handed. What I discovered was something quite the contrary. Death gave me permission to start over, to abandon everything I had previously known in my faith journey, and to set out to discover a God greater than my grief.

The reason I am writing now is to share the God revealed. Not that I won't always continue learning and knowing God, but the last brush strokes on this particular canvas, the one revealing a real peace within loss, has now occurred. My soul has acquitted this One I placed on trial. In fact, my soul, seized by the power of a great affection, has found this blameless One to be the answer to any lasting joy and peace I can have this side of heaven.

I have witnessed Jesus cry with me and for me, and I have seen Him dance and cradle my daughter in His arms, and I have watched angels tend to her. I have seen God's face and have felt Him cup my own with His hands. He is loving-kindness. He is beautiful. He is strong, and He is trustworthy. I've learned that He will *transform your valley of trouble into a gateway of hope (Hosea 2:15 NLT)*. He will lead you through the dark cemetery of your life to discover a valley with green pastures and a spring of living water to restore you and to remind you that eternity is waiting for you. No matter how bereaved your soul or fragile your existence, Jesus is friend and counselor, but He is also champion and God Almighty. If you have ever suffered so deeply that you were afraid you wouldn't be able to catch your next breath, then let this testimony speak comfort and truth to your wounded soul and let Him offer you His hand of redemption, for *A bruised reed He will not break, a smoldering wick He will not snuff out. In faithfulness He will bring forth justice (Isaiah 42:3)*.

This is the Jesus of my grief...

# CHAPTER 2

# GIFTS OF GRIEF

*"Every good and perfect gift is from above coming
down from the father of heavenly lights, who
does not change like shifting shadows."*

*James 1:17*

Simple white fabric with tiny, vibrant flowers of red, yellow, and blue were speckled across the dress that clothed the little girl. Her light auburn hair fell into braids on either side of her delighted face and rested upon her pleated sleeves. She skipped joyfully in a field of tall grass unaware of anything but the sunlight and the meadow. She circled until she came up to me as if pausing purposefully for a moment. "Hi mommy," she said with a wave of simplicity as if she had said it and would say it a million times more. "Hi sweetie," was my desperate but controlled reply. Without hesitation, she skipped off into the distance.

This was my first vision of Anna, my first peek behind the curtain into an unreachable but real world of permanence. If I could just somehow freeze time and live within our sweet and comfortable exchange forever. To open my eyes would awaken me to the bright lights and sounds of a hospital room and the delivery of death into my trembling arms. But seeing her and hearing her even for that brief moment gave me the courage to move forward without complete trepidation to behold the daughter her father and I had conceived and adored. The image of her delight and her definite knowledge and affection for me, her mother, momentarily inflated my collapsing spirit. The vision was the first of many holy handprints.

From the moment we learned of Anna's death, God went before us and pressed many more tangible signs of His presence into the sad reality we would endure. Each of these encounters I came to think of as a gift of grief. These moments reminded me that the Jesus I would begin to form impressions of, and often accuse, was not entirely the villain my heart condemned.

## A FOREVER HEARTBEAT

I knew that the moment I gave birth, the countdown to letting Anna go would begin. Somehow staying pregnant was a consolation. We learned of Anna's death on a Tuesday night. My sister Kristen rushed to the hospital, stayed with us during those first terrifying hours of grief, and then drove us home at about 2:00 AM.

Walking into the house meant embracing the first of many realizations of loss. I went directly to the nursery. Chris had cautiously asked me if he should close the door, but I wanted to face it head on. As I walked into the room, my eyes locked on the soft, pink, contoured pillow I had dreamed of cradling Anna on as I nursed her. I began weeping, my knees buckling beneath the weight of grief, and I had to grab the dresser to keep from falling. I was so weak I could barely stand. I reached to turn on the lamp that I had turned on every morning before, with a joyful, "Good-morning Anna girl. We can't wait to meet you," and the light bulb instantly blew out. It was as if her nursery knew what was taking place and had therefore turned out its light of life as well. I felt terrified by the darkness and irony.

Chris and I each took a sleeping pill that the nurse had given us and slept for a couple of hours before the sun came up and reminded us that our lives had fallen apart. I was crying and in Chris's arms before I took my first cognitive breath. "Hold her," I said. I wanted to be a family so desperately. I wanted her daddy to love her and to touch her like he had every night and every morning for months. As we lay there together I was very aware of my agony for Chris. Nearly nine months had made him a daddy, and now there would be no baby to lavish that love upon. I was sick with empathy.

Family poured in one by one that day. Each person brought us to new depths in our loss as I imagined what their relationship with Anna might have been. She wasn't just ours. She would have become theirs as well. That evening we headed back to the hospital to begin the induction of labor, which was an extremely long and exhausting process. The length, however, bought us time which I was extremely grateful for. It had been twenty-four hours of suffering, and it had felt like an eternity. The grief had only just begun. How would we endure the next few days? That was Wednesday evening. Anna didn't come into the world until Friday at 11:45 AM. During those hours, friends and family camped out in the waiting room and took turns sitting at my bedside. Each friend brought new waves of tears and comfort. In the middle of the night, just ten hours before Anna was born, I woke up, suddenly remembering what has since served to be one of the most precious gifts of grief.

"Chris, wake up!" He jumped up and rushed to my side. He was so afraid. "We have her heartbeat!" I started to cry. It was the most energy and joy I had felt in days. Chris was clearly confused. "We have her heartbeat," I desperately, joyfully said again.

The Pregnancy Center had made a documentary a few months earlier to be shown at churches in order to promote our work. We wanted to be able to show area churches exactly what we were all about, extending the love and truth of God to women in crisis and their unborn babies. The videographer had really wanted to record an ultrasound of an expecting client, and when I was asked to be the actress, I had joyfully agreed.

When I remembered that we had a visual record of her life, I felt an inkling of happiness and relief for the first time in days. You can't imagine the ecstasy I felt knowing I would be able to watch and hear her heart beating and see her little legs kicking anytime I wanted. It was proof that she had existed and evidence of the very intimate and beautiful relationship we had already shared. The role for which she had been cast had allowed her the opportunity to reveal God's creative power and the reality of life in the womb. I was overcome with gratitude and pride.

I pushed the nurse call button, and Alice rushed into the room. I suppose I had scared her as well. "Alice I have a video, a video of Anna, her heartbeat, her face, her body…I have a record." Alice gently wiped the tears from my face and the hair off my brow and smiled. She encouraged me to go back to sleep, but I could not rest. I couldn't wait for my family to come the next day so I could let them know, that they could see a day when their granddaughter and their niece had lived. My brother David took this footage along with video from the day she was born and compiled it together into a remarkable tribute. It is a beautiful and sacred portrait of our daughter. It is a gift our entire family cherishes, a forever heartbeat, the testimony of life and the reminder of what was and is to come.

## MY HERO...OUR PARTNER

Dr. Jeanne O'Nan was one of the obstetricians at my doctor's office, and she was also the Medical Director at the Crisis Pregnancy Center. She, as well as my nurse mid-wife Beth Broderson, volunteered at the center and shared our heart and mission for unborn babies, yet I didn't know Jeanne very well. She was also pregnant, about six weeks farther along and expecting twins. I knew she would be on maternity leave when I was due, so I had been seeing the nurse mid-wife. When Anna died, Beth was undergoing cancer treatments in Texas, and Jeanne was at home with her twin boys. I was a stranger to everyone else.

The director of the pregnancy center called Jeanne at home to let her know what had happened, and she immediately came to see me. I started weeping when she walked into the room. She sat down on my bed, held my hand, and treated me as a suffering friend. Jeanne was a doctor who fully understood. She had already endured a similar loss with another patient the year before. She asked me if I wanted her to deliver Anna. Through tears and speechlessness, I nodded yes.

Jeanne instructed the nurses to call her at home when it was close to the time of delivery. It was taking forever to get to the end, but when it happened, it happened quickly. The nurses had called Jeanne, but prepared me that they didn't think she would make it in time. I was preparing to push with the nurse who had called another doctor from the practice to come deliver our baby. I felt so afraid. Everything was happening so fast. I felt like such a number. As I took a deep breath to begin the first push, Jeanne ran through the door.

I didn't have to push long, and then I heard it, "She's beautiful." Jeanne was crying as she held my daughter in her arms and told me what I saw to be true with my own eyes. She was beautiful, she looked like me, and she was dead.

I watched as Anna was cared for by our precious nurse Alice, and as her daddy studied her adoringly with a smile I had never before seen on his face. He was in awe of her. Meeting her and seeing her was such a thrill; it was as if we forgot our reality for a moment. And then they placed her in my arms for what would be the sweetest and most painful moment of my life.

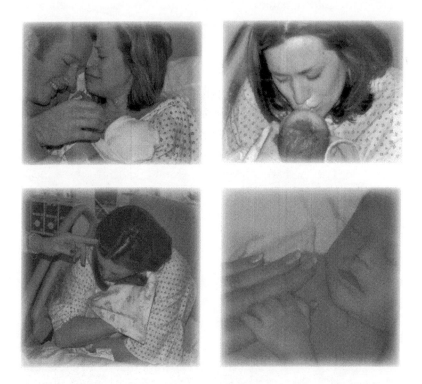

Taking her in was so exhilarating, so agonizing. As I smothered her with my tears, my love, and my kisses, Jeanne sat on my bed, placed her head on my shoulder, and whispered, "I am going to deliver so many more babies for you. You will have another baby in your arms this time next year." It was a statement of hope. Her confidence and her, "I'm in this with you" attitude made me feel as if we had a comrade in the fight. It was a bold prophecy. Dr. Jeanne O'Nan was truly an impression of the kind hand of God.

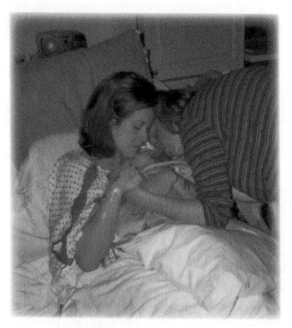

*Kate, Anna and Dr. Jeanne O'nan*

## INSTRUMENTS OF PEACE

My sister is five years older than I am and my dearest friend. Kristen opened the maternal room in my heart in 1999 when my first niece Rebekah was born. Oh, how I adored her. My arms ached for hours each time I left her and ached until I would hold her again. Two years later, there was Sarah, and two years after that, there was Bethy. When Beth was a few days old, God spoke a beautiful phrase to Kristen about Beth. He said, "She will be an instrument of peace." When Kristen shared this with me, I felt a growing anticipation in my heart that Beth could be God's answer to the peace we had so often prayed for in Kristen's life. As Beth grew and the difficult circumstances remained, it seemed God's promise would be unfulfilled. When Kristen placed her

18-month-old Beth in my grieving arms, we realized that she was *my* instrument of peace. I will never forget that moment.

Chris and I poured every ounce of stored-up parenting love into Bethy. Kristen and my brother- in-law Mike were so gracious to let us take many of their moments and make them ours. Their house became ours too. Our home was a reminder of what we didn't have, and the fullness and opportunities of Kristen's home provided safe distractions. Rebekah and Sarah were old enough to understand and to be sad. They were also instruments of God's love for us. Five-year-old Sarah kept a tissue, a flower, and a picture of Jesus with children on his lap in a drawer in the living room. Every time she saw me crying she would rush to the drawer, fling it open, and bombard me with her heartfelt remedies and a hug.

During the first few hours we were home from the hospital, I was sitting on the sofa with my whole family encircling me. Five-year-old Sarah walked across the room and put a cold washcloth against my cheek. "Feel this, Dee-Dee" she said. She crossed the room to come to me. She didn't choose anyone else for this strange gesture. The coldness of the washcloth was exactly the same coldness of sweet Anna's face that I had pressed against my own just hours before. It was a supernatural act of God's loving kindness. I believe that in that moment, God extended a gift to remind me—heavy with the pain of wanting and needing what I couldn't have—exactly how Anna's face had felt. It became a ritual for Chris and me to deliberately place cold things on our faces, closing our eyes and remembering. Through our tears, we would smile and say, "Anna cold."

My nieces have continued to be instruments of God's peace as I miss my own expression of femininity. They continue to ask, to remember, and to celebrate Anna's life. They were, and indeed continue to be, lovely gifts of grief.

*Kate with Rebekah, Sarah and Beth*

# ANNA ROSE KATHERINE

When I first found out we were pregnant, I began to pray that God would give me a special prayer specific for the baby He was growing inside of me. I prayed many things for her, but I'll never forget the moment when I heard the Lord speak to my heart, "child of worship." I remember thinking what a specific and beautiful prayer that was. It's a prayer that, without prompting, I never would have prayed. And so it became my greatest and most fervent prayer for our baby. As soon as we found out we were having a girl, the list of names began compiling itself in our minds as we sought to select the one most perfect for her. We had five names on the list. Then it occurred to us that God might already have a name picked out for our baby, so we began to pray that He would reveal it to us. One day I was reading in my Bible, and I came across this scripture...

*Anna, a prophetess was also there in the temple. She never left there day and night worshipping God with fasting and prayer. She came along just as Simeon was talking with Mary and Joseph, and she began praising God. She talked about the child to everyone who had been waiting expectantly for God to rescue Jerusalem. (Luke 2:36-38 NLT).*

When I read this scripture it clicked. It was as if God had handed me a piece of paper upon which Anna's name was written. As an answer to the specific prayer God had laid on my heart, finally "our baby" became "our Anna."

My prayer developed more and more for her, and I prayed that she would become a "baby of worship," that in a supernatural way she would be able to understand what it meant to love Jesus, to adore Him, and to accept His love for her. As Anna grew in my womb, it was confirmed for us over and over that we had chosen the right name. She squirmed the most and kicked the hardest during worship at church and when I would sing to her. Anna was delighted by worship. As a matter of fact, in the last two weeks of her life while I was sick, I had lost my voice and wasn't able to sing to her. I will never forget getting in my car after not driving for sixteen days and how Anna rolled and grooved when I turned on the familiar worship music. She had missed it. God had already answered my prayer. Anna was a baby of worship, and she was already delighting her mother and her heavenly Father with her expressions of praise.

The morning of her memorial service, I was writing a statement to be read, and it occurred to me that Anna had come into the fullness of my prayer for her. Now I realize that God had not only intended it as a prayer, but He had also whispered to me what He already knew her future would soon become. I don't know exactly what Anna's days look like, but I know that every single one of them is filled with worshiping God. I said it on the day of her service, and I will say it again now. I couldn't be prouder of my daughter who is singing her praises to Jesus, just like her namesake Anna did in the temple…all day and all night.

## POWER IN A NAME

When I was in college, I spent a summer with Campus Crusade for Christ in Minsk, Belarus. I will never forget meeting Nastya. She had a serene and magnetic quality. I adored her from the moment I met her and wanted to be part of her life. Nastya let me teach her about Jesus during the summer of 2000, and He rescued her soul.

When I met Nastya, I asked her a question that I have never asked anyone before. Even as I heard myself ask it, I was completely taken aback. "What does your name mean?" She explained, "Nastya is a nickname for Annastacia." She began to motion with her hands, a sweeping upward, and then she said, "I am to do what Jesus Christ did." She paused for a moment as she was trying to remember her English vocabulary, and then she said, "I am to rise." I was overwhelmed. This precious girl's only knowledge of Christ was through the meaning of her name. Her very name held the secret power of God, the essence of the Gospel, and she didn't even know it. As I settled into my bed that night, I prayed for sweet Annastacia, that she would indeed rise like Christ.

It had been years since I had seen Nastya, but still, I loved her deeply. As I thought about our first encounter, hands resting on my swollen stomach, it dawned on me that Anna was the first part of her given name. How perfect to honor Nastya and to give our baby a name connected to such a beautiful word and experience: resurrection.

One afternoon, love sick and grieving, I began to write her beautiful name down again and again. As I wrote and meditated on what each part of her name meant and why we had chosen Anna Rose, a revelation fell upon me. The name Anna means grace, and of course as I have already shared, Anna the prophetess was a worshipper I prayed for my Anna to be. Rose was Chris's paternal grandmother who passed away right before we married. Katherine is my given name which we added after learning she had slipped away from us. I wanted to send a part of myself with her. Katherine means "pure one." So there I sat staring at her name and each meaning: Anna – child of worship, grace, resurrection; Rose – a heavenly grandmother, past tense of rise; Katherine – pure one.

The words slowly came together, and this sentence came tumbling from my hand:

> Anna Rose Katherine, my **child of worship,** who, by **grace, rose** to **purity.**

Jesus knew what would take place. He gave me the fullness of her name as a gift of grief to hold onto once we learned what He already knew. Her very name is a sentence describing her rich destiny in Christ.

Parents pray for certain things to be fulfilled for their children all their lives: salvation, safety, success, a husband or wife, healthy children…on and on. God gave me eight and a half months to pray for the one thing I can absolutely say I know has been fulfilled in her life. She is a child of worship, she is resurrected, and she is pure. Anna's name is a precious gift of grief.

## ANNA'S SONG

I love to sing, and I wanted to write a lullaby for Anna. Just six weeks before she died, these were the words that came together as I rocked in her nursery.

> Baby girl, baby girl, can you see?
> The Father's love is pouring down on thee.
> Baby girl, baby girl, can you hear?
> Rushing water, angels everywhere.
> You were created in His image, knitted in my womb.
> With His finger, He'll touch that smile upon your face.
> Baby girl, baby girl, Can you feel?
> The hug of heaven, my womb around your shape.

I am so grateful God prompted me with these words for Anna. I was given an opportunity to tell her about the home where she would be spending her life. I sang to her about my womb hugging her body, a foreshadowing of the hug and warmth of heaven itself. I sang about the Father's love, the sound of angels, and the touch of God's finger to put a smile upon her little face. How very true the words have become. Anna's song *is* Anna's life.

The gifts of Anna's name and Anna's song are gifts of motherhood. I will never be able to tell Anna about what to expect in kindergarten, how to tie her shoes, or how to mend a broken heart. I was able to tell her about heaven though, and this is a gift that far surpasses the ability to pass on sewing or a sense of style. For all the things I didn't get to do, the one I did was tremendous. God gave that to me supernaturally. In His foreknowledge, He was so kind. Anna's song is yet another precious gift of grief.

From February 22, 2005 to the present, Chris and I have thought about these gifts again and again. I have rehearsed their meaning repeatedly in my heart and mind, and I am abundantly grateful. But…the story doesn't end here.

Though the gifts were sweet, they couldn't erase the bitter journey of grief that was waiting to be embarked upon everyday. The flip side of the goodness of these gifts was the pain of the fact that God knew. In essence, that is what each gift was saying to me. They were puzzle pieces fitting together, forming in my mind the face of an omniscient and seemingly dispassionate and uncaring God. Why hadn't He stopped it? How in the world could I rely upon His love and comfort with His sovereignty hanging in the air like an enormous lightning bolt over my life? He allowed this suffering to come upon us. For me, God's sovereignty and His kindness in the knowing threatened the reality of His love. It was time to let the volcano of anger erupt and to face it head on.

Accusations rose loud and clear from the depths of my soul, and they scared me. As I prayed, "Lord, use this to make me better and not bitter, and Lord help me to grieve in a holy way," I heard whispers rumbling deep inside me, words of hatred directed toward the Savior of my youth. I knew a war was on the horizon, and excruciating days were ahead.

A new part of the journey was now beginning, the long road to discovering the Jesus of my Grief.

# PART TWO

# JESUS

# CHAPTER 3

# FACE TO FACE

*For these things I weep; my eyes overflow with tears, because a comforter, one who could refresh and restore my soul is far from me. My children are perishing for the enemy has prevailed...You have bereaved my soul and cast it off far from peace. I have forgotten what goodness and happiness are.*

*Lamentations 1:16, 3:17 (AMP)*

*I will not leave you orphans, I will come to you.*

*John 14:18*

I'll never forget the first moment I saw Jesus. My mother was praying for me as I lay on my bed, a depressed sixteen-year-old girl. I didn't want her to pray. I was irritated by her holy attempt to fix me. But as she prayed, something to the effect of, "knowing Jesus was present with us," I saw Him. He didn't say anything, He was just there. I remember cupping my hand over my mouth so the laughter wouldn't escape as my sweet mother continued praying. I assumed my imagination had gotten the better of me. But when I couldn't imagine Jesus away and peace invaded the room, I knew He was there.

Sometimes I close my eyes and try to imagine Jesus in a certain situation and what He might say or do. But at other times, I see Him, and it's nothing I create or conjure up. He just appears. As I close my eyes, it's like the dark in a theatre just before the big picture begins to play. Then I see Him standing there, visions of the Savior, like waking dreams.

During the second trimester of my pregnancy, I learned of a prominent Christian therapist, Stephen Johnson, who was offering classes on a method of healing prayer. It was a Christ-centered counseling approach to therapy I had heard about and was eager to learn. I wanted to be able to minister effectively to my clients at the pregnancy center. The therapist teaching the classes had witnessed tremendous healing and freedom for his clients by intentionally providing an opening for Jesus to reveal Himself as the great counselor and healer He promises to be. Over and over again, he had witnessed *the* light appearing and healing places once dark with pain.

While taking the classes, I offered to be a guinea pig for the students to witness how this type of prayer ministry could be demonstrated in one's life. I hadn't intended to volunteer, but I felt so prompted by God that I knew I had to raise my hand when the request was made. There was a particular painful moment in my childhood that continued to plague me, and I was desperate for freedom. I shared the memory out loud, tears streaming down my face. The counselor responded by simply asking Jesus to give me His healing truth, whatever that truth might be. God answered that prayer when I saw Jesus. My eyes were opened to where He had been on that dreadful day twenty years before:

> Jesus held out His hand, just as I imagine He did when He rebuked the wind and the waves, silencing painful words spoken by another who had wrongfully accused and shamed me. At Jesus' gesture, my accuser was hardened like stone. I watched in amazement as Jesus took a chisel and shattered the statue, thus breaking the power of His speech and subsequent lies. I ran past the broken fragments of the memory which lay on the

ground beneath me and into Christ's outstretched arms. He then whispered into my ear sacred words, truth that healed me and set me free from the grip of deceit and its accompanying pain.

I sat there weeping along with the rest of the class as Jesus had visually presented Himself to me as a healer of the pain that had been stored in this memory. I had seen His face, I had heard His voice, and healing had taken place. The evidence was the peace that was given to me in exchange for the shame I had carried for twenty years.

Following Anna's death, it was an easy decision to pursue prayer counseling for my grief. I picked up the phone just three weeks after our loss to call the counselor. Through a torrent of tears, I told him what had happened and asked if it was too soon to come to him for help. He answered that it would be too soon for some things but not for others.

It had been three weeks since the day I learned of Anna's death in my womb, and for three weeks I clung to God. I knew I needed Him to survive. I had enough history with Him and enough belief in Him to know cognitively and somewhat experientially that He would be my sustainer and comforter. For this reason I suppressed every ounce of anger and every theological question that plagued my heart and mind. My sister was the only one brave enough to reach in and give me permission to air my true feelings. "Kate, are you angry with God? I would be. It's understandable if you feel that way." But I wouldn't do it. If I were to open the lid on the doubt that swelled beneath the surface, I knew my fury would erupt in a plume of smoke, obscuring any remnant of God's beauty from my view.

As I sat in the waiting room, I felt so scared. I contemplated the spiritual torment that lay waiting to emerge. I desperately wanted Jesus to reveal Himself to me, yet I was terrified of what I might say or do if He did. I was hungry for His love and furious at Him for allowing tragedy to enter my life. I hadn't even verbalized to Chris my spiritual turmoil. I knew that once I let it out, I would never be able to retrieve the words. I was reluctant to let anyone witness the weeping and grief I knew would come. But I couldn't heal by myself. I needed an aid to help me sort through the debris and put things back in place. Would I ever love and trust God again, or was I doomed to be committed to a god I didn't like? Would I ever feel happy again, or would the sadness consume every inch of my heart and mind for a lifetime? Was I stuck in this valley of despair, or was there a way forward, albeit a narrow and hard way?

I took a seat on a leather couch as I prepared to take the first step into the journey of healing I was both ready and reluctant to begin. I didn't know where to start, and my throat was aching from holding back the floodgate of emotion. I opened my mouth, and it all came tumbling forth. The hour was quickly filled with a million words of sorrow and tears as I shared my tragedy and bared my wounded soul to my counselor.

At the end of the hour, I felt gravely disappointed that I would be walking out of his office no better than when I had entered. I was exhausted and limp. I knew I couldn't do this week after week. I needed something more. Not grieving advice, not professional jargon. I needed something better than good grief; I needed something great.

The therapist offered his tender words of empathy and informed me that there was no quick path through grief. It would simply take the time that it would take. Then he prayed for me. After several minutes, he simply asked God a question. He paused for God to answer as if he knew for certain that He would. "Jesus, what is the one thing you want Kate to know before she leaves here today?" I sat for a moment contemplating his confidence, afraid I might disappoint his expectations. The screen of my mind was blank. And then suddenly, there was light.

> I turned with the eyes of my heart to find Jesus sitting on the far left-hand side of the leather couch with one cushion vacant between us. Then I noticed that His hand was extended, palm upward across the empty seat. I was afraid to look directly at His face. I wasn't sure I was ready to take hold of all His offer meant.

I opened my eyes and sat for a moment, stunned by what I had just seen. The counselor asked me to explain what was going on. I described the image of Christ, and then I said, "I think He wants me to hold His hand." His response was a simple question, "Do you want to?" My initial thought was, "Do I have a choice?"

To accept His hand would concede acceptance and intimacy I didn't think I was ready for. I needed to fight with this God, and holding His hand wouldn't allow me the space I needed to figure Him out. Yet there was a clear whisper from within my heart, the unaffected child in me that pleaded, "Look at Him." After a brief moment of contemplation, I submitted to her and reluctantly turned and shifted my gaze to meet Jesus. He said nothing, but the look in His eyes said a million "somethings" of love.

It was the first time I had seen His face and heard His voice since my life and dreams had shattered into a thousand pieces. I wish I could adequately describe the look He gave and the fire it ignited in my soul, melting layers of my reserve. The best words I can find are loving kindness. There was a tender ownership in His gaze that pierced my heart and reminded me that Jesus was not my enemy.

Again, I noticed His hand, and this time I accepted His invitation. As our hands met, He declared, "I'm not going anywhere." The statement was calm but sure. He spoke as if He were saying it for the second time, like a reminder of a promise already made. "I'm not going anywhere," signaled that I hadn't been abandoned by God and that He didn't plan on leaving anytime soon. My heart's inquisition and anger had not sent Him running for the hills. He was promising to stay put. Jesus hadn't gone anywhere.

Once more, I explained to the therapist everything that had taken place in my mind. I was smiling in disbelief and amazement at this supernatural encounter that had provided me with the remnant of faith I needed to receive anew God's love toward me. It had given me the opportunity to reach out to Jesus. We were going to be okay. There was a long road ahead, but we would make it. He wasn't going anywhere, and to my surprise, I was desperately in need of that promise. My mind and heart were fighting, but my soul and the Spirit within me were crying to belong to God.

Jesus spoke similar words to His dearest friends on the night before the most excruciating tragedy they would ever face. He said to them, *I will not leave you as orphans, I will come to you (John 14:18)*. This was one of the last promises Jesus spoke to His followers before His death. It was an essential truth to write on their hearts before they endured unthinkable grief. Would they also struggle? Would they also feel like Jesus had abandoned them? Did He know this?

"I will be with you!" Again, Jesus spoke these words after His resurrection and after he spent forty more days with the disciples before He went to sit at the right hand of His Father. He said, *Surely I am with you always, to the very end of the age (Matthew 28:20)*. Twice, He reassured His friends of His omnipresence, directly before and directly after His death.

Brennan Manning is a Christian author who has greatly impacted my faith. In his book Abba's Child, he shares his profound insights on Matthew 28:20 and the promise of presence from the lips of Jesus:

> Limiting the resurrection either to the past or to the future makes the present risenness of Jesus largely irrelevant, safeguards us from interference with the ordinary rounds and daily routine of our lives, and preempts communion now with Jesus as a living person. In other words, the resurrection needs to be experienced as present risenness. If we take seriously the words of the risen Christ, *Know that I am with you always; yes, to the end of time (Matthew 28:20)*, we should expect that He will be actively present in our lives. If our faith is alive and luminous, we will be alert to moments, events and occasions when the power of the resurrection is brought to bear on our lives. Self-absorbed and inattentive, we fail to notice the subtle ways Jesus is snagging our attention.[1]

The assurance of Christ's presence was the primary truth His disciples needed. The same was true for me. It was the first stone to be laid on the road to recovering the face of God. It was also the last thing Jesus spoke to His disciples before He ascended into heaven.

There was another beautiful truth of Christ I absorbed that day. Jesus is a gentleman. He could have sat right next to me on the couch and grabbed my hand, but He didn't. He knew that trust had been lost and that there was distance between us.

---

[1]  Brennan Manning, Abba's Child; The Cry of the Heart for Intimate Belonging (Colorado Springs: NavPress,1994), p102.

Instead of breaking boundaries and forcing Himself on me, He gave me the choice to accept the invitation of His hand.

The first step had been successfully taken. I grieved, I was exhausted, and truth had found its way into my aching heart. As I stood to leave, I knew that Jesus had stood as well. The sense was so real that I literally turned to look behind me. The vision wasn't simply a self-conjured happy idea to appease my orphaned heart. Christ had been in that room, and He planned on going with me.

He was still the Jesus of my pain, my anger, my doubt and confusion, but He had just become the Jesus of permanent presence. Another brush stroke had been painted by God's perfect hand. I cried the whole way home. I ached for Anna. I was still utterly confused and hurt by God's allowance of tragedy. But there was hope: Jesus wasn't going anywhere.

# CHAPTER 4

# MY KIND OF GAL

*This then is how we know we belong to the truth
and how we set our hearts at rest in his presence
whenever our hearts condemn us, For God is greater
than our hearts and He knows everything.*

1st John 3:19-20

*Let us then approach the throne of grace with
confidence, so that we may receive mercy and
find grace to help us in our time of need.*

Hebrews 4:16

A week slowly passed. The sun rose each day urging us to get out of bed. Each morning I cursed the sun. Sleep became a dear friend, a break, unless it was filled with nightmares, as it often was. Through each grievous moment of the day, I replayed my encounter a week earlier with the risen and present Jesus.

I was ready to go back to counseling. Admittedly, I was nervous about how God might present Himself, and nervous that He wouldn't present Himself at all. I recognized the vision as a gift. I knew I wasn't in control of it and was curious to see if the Jesus movie that had spontaneously appeared in my mind was a one-time gift, or if God would continue to push play. There was something new to report. There was a heavy weight on my heart and mind, and it was making me feel ill. It was guilt.

I felt guilty about everything. I felt guilty that my body had failed my baby. The autopsy came back with nothing to report. Had it been a fluke, an accident, an Almighty "oops?" There was no answer. I was either pointing the finger at God or at myself. Both accounts of blame left me paralyzed with guilt, one leading to anger; the other to inconsolable sadness. I felt guilty that I wasn't able to sustain Anna and guilty that I wasn't feeling the way a Christian should feel. Who was I to express anything but gratitude to God? He had rescued me from Hell, and this is how I was repaying Him. We were not equals, but I was certainly acting like He owed me something.

Just moments before Anna's lifeless body was taken from my arms forever, I said to Chris, "This isn't right!" Chris looked at me as tenderly as he ever has and said, "Sweets, the most unfair thing that ever happened was Jesus dying on the cross for our sins." He was right. Truly the most unfair thing that ever happened was the death of pure Christ for wretched me. Chris handed me the perfect trump card for the awfulness and unfairness of the hand we were dealt. But how could he say such holy things and exemplify such trust? I was an ungrateful hypocrite, and I hated myself for it. I couldn't make the feelings go away. Rage existed right alongside my need for God. I was a mess.

As I sat on the leather couch and unpacked my guilt, the counselor simply said, "God, what do you have to say about that?" as if he were the mediator in a counseling session with two people. He closed his eyes and tilted his head as if listening, so I followed his lead. Eyes closed, I saw Him before even a moment had elapsed.

As I rocked in Anna's vacant nursery, tears streaming down my face, Jesus knelt before me crying. His lips were moving, but I couldn't hear anything He was saying.

Frustrated at my deafness, I opened my eyes and relayed my vision to the counselor. He prayed that I would be able to hear the words Jesus was speaking. As I closed my eyes, I was immediately back in the nursery.

As Jesus spoke, His words seemed like a vapor that silently left His lips and hit an invisible wall between us. "What was the wall?" I wondered. Something was keeping me from hearing His voice. He was crying, overcome with sadness. I could tell that whatever He was saying He desperately wanted me to hear.

Then I heard a noise behind me. I turned toward the noise, and my eyes were drawn into a memory that I hadn't thought of in years. I was seven years old and standing in the kitchen of my childhood home. My father was standing across the room, singing me his signature song. "My kind of gal, Katie is. She's got the bluest eyes. She's got the sweetest smile. My kind of gal, Katie is…" You would think I would be touched and delighted by his song of affection. But I was furious. I can't remember the reason, but I was extremely angry about something he had or hadn't done. His playful and tender attempts were not softening my heart. He came across the room, took me in his arms, and began dancing with me, singing over and over, "My kind of gal, Katie is." I was screaming for him to stop singing and was trying to free myself from his grip. And then I started hitting him. Over and over I beat his chest with my tiny, raging fists. The memory was a perfect account of what had taken place eighteen years earlier.

I opened my eyes and began to inform the counselor of what had occurred in the silence. He encouraged me to go back into the memory to learn if there was anything else Jesus wanted me to see. As I closed my eyes, the image of me beating my father continued.

I tilted my head which was buried in his chest to look up at his face. To my surprise, I was not in my father's clutch. It was Jesus I was hitting. Unaffected by my aggression, He tenderly swayed and sang, "My kind of gal, Katie is," while I unleashed my fury on Him.

I'd had enough. I couldn't see anymore. I opened my eyes, and it was a few moments before I could speak. I was devastated with embarrassment. How could I verbalize what I had witnessed? God knew the anger I harbored toward Him. He had found me out. Now there was nowhere to hide. I had to say it out loud for the therapist to hear, and worst of all, for me to hear.

Was God patronizing me? Was He using this childhood memory to acquaint me with my sinfulness? Now I really felt guilty. I finally mustered up the courage needed to fully expose myself and shared every humiliating detail. With a deep sigh of shame, I looked up to see my counselor, eyes filled with tears, a drop of tenderness upon his cheek. Did he understand that God was seeking to expose the extent of my sinfulness? The counselor could tell I was confused by his response, so he said,

"Kate, do you understand what God is saying to you? You are His kind of gal." I sat there for a moment and then he said, "You need to let this soak in."

I sat quietly pondering his analysis. His words perched for a moment on top of my hard heart and then with one fell swoop swept through my soul with perfect clarity. I saw everything the way God intended it and not the way my guilt had interpreted it. God wasn't seeking to show me the extent of my anger in order to inflict further shame and guilt upon me. He was seeking to show me the extent of His love in the midst of my anger, to *alleviate* my shame and guilt.

God had taken me back to one of my earliest memories of being angry at my earthly father. It was the perfect childhood memory to parallel my current feelings toward my heavenly Father. My dad was determined to love me regardless of my feelings or actions toward him. Fathers love their daughters no matter what! Could God possibly be communicating such adoration and acceptance to wretched, ungrateful me? Was I truly His kind of gal? Did He really like me that much?

Somewhere along the way I had adopted a performance-based theology in my relationship with God. I knew this was something I'd been struggling with, but I had not realized how deeply my feelings were embedded in my heart. I instantly felt flooded with warmth. I wanted to cry, but I wasn't sure why. My soul had already registered what my mind had not yet conceived. The God of the Universe adored me. I was His child, and my adoption as His daughter meant loving me no matter what. The guilt I had felt for not measuring up was vanishing.

Can you see the prodigal son on the horizon, his Father waiting for him? Can you hear the wayward son's pounding heart as fear surges through his veins? Can you hear the questions of his soul? Will he still love me? Will he accept me? Will he acknowledge me? *I'll ask him if he will let me be one of his hired servants.* Can you hear his guilt? I can. *And yet, while he was a still long way off, his Father ran to him (Luke 15:11-31).* This is how it is with our heavenly Father: unconditional, relentless, and measureless love.

Tears streaked my face as I felt more loved by God that ever before. Change was occurring at the core of my soul, and I could feel it pressing outward. This love would eventually permeate each layer until I was free. I sensed it. I couldn't speak, but the expression on my face spoke through the tears. The counselor now urged me to close my eyes and to enter the childhood memory again.

> I saw a seven-year-old little girl running at break-neck speed across the room into her Savior's arms. He laughed and smiled and continued singing and swaying as she buried her head in His chest. The little girl who had used anger to assure safety finally surrendered herself to her Father's affections.

The image shifted and I found myself sitting in Anna's nursery again.

> Jesus was still sitting at my feet crying, but this time I could hear His voice. His words vibrated with tenderness, and with the fullness of His own grief He uttered, "I am so sorry." He bowed his head and continued weeping.

The moment connected me to Mary and Martha as they too watched Jesus weep at the death of their dear brother Lazarus. In that grievous moment centuries ago, Jesus had wept for His own pain; He wept for Mary and Martha, and now He wept for me. My heart softened and crumbled under Christ's partnership in my pain, and I went to Him.

One hour had transformed me. So much healing had taken place. My mind and my heart felt release. I could barely put into words what had happened, but as I continued to meditate on my experience with Jesus, healing flowed through me and greater understanding as well.

My guilt was the poisonous fruit of believing the lie that I must be perfect in order to come to God. The wall that kept me from hearing the voice of Jesus was this lie, my self-righteousness which was barring me from the truth. So God took me through a back door to hear the truth, the door of a memory. I was God's kind of gal, no matter what my feelings were. Once I realized this truth, my mind was free from the guilt it had endured. My worth and acceptance were no longer based upon my performance. The truth didn't make my anger disappear, but it did give me permission to be angry with the promise that God's love for me is unconditional. His feelings for me weren't contingent upon my behavior. My spirit, grateful for a new way to approach God, ran to Him in gratitude. Now the wall had collapsed, and I could hear the message Christ had come to give – a message of compassion. He met me in the nursery, the room of my suffering, and offered me a two-thousand-year-old gift. *Jesus wept,* and I embraced it (John 11:35). My soul had been so parched for God's tears. His grief had quenched my thirst for holy compssion.

God's truth won another room in my heart that day. The theology of grace was being written on my soul. If we were going to build a new relationship, the foundation had to be firm. The cornerstone is grace. It is Jesus. *Let us then approach the throne of grace with confidence, that we may receive mercy and find help in our time of need (Hebrews 4:16)*. God was reminding me that I could approach Him with confidence because of His grace poured over me. In other words, come boldly into God's presence, no matter how miserable and despicable you feel. There will be a fresh batch of mercy waiting for you whenever you need it. The cause of my guilt was the shame I felt for my angry attitude toward God. Now I was free to deal honestly with God, free from guilt. I was acceptable, not because I was perfect, but because He is, and I belonged to Him.

I began to let myself function in grace and no longer in the suffocating system of performance. Understanding my worth in Christ released me from needing to obtain it in any other way. Performance had been driving my friendships as well. So many of my thoughts were consumed with fear over whom I may have disappointed since my life had shattered. I felt guilty for not returning calls, guilty for not being able to be close to friends who were reveling in the joys of new motherhood. With a new awareness of God's heart for me, I had permission from the Lord and myself to approach life and relationships in a whole new way. It was time to be free.

## TIME TO BE HONEST

The session was coming to a close, but there was still one more step to take. In recognizing that I could come boldly before God's throne of grace, it was time to do just that. It was important for me to acknowledge aloud my lack of trust and the distance I felt toward God. I felt undeniable peace, but I was still very aware of my overall anger at God and my definite lack of trust in Him. I told the counselor how confused I was that I could still be feeling such anger and distrust, having so profoundly experienced Christ's love. I told him how much I wanted Jesus yet how I wanted to keep Him at a distance. I didn't trust Him yet. I still felt betrayed.

I was completely taken back when the therapist asked me to tell Jesus that I wasn't going to trust Him right now. Can a Christian say such a thing? Would lightning bolts fall from the sky? But with the lesson of coming boldly before God's throne fresh under my belt, I went to Jesus and simply said, "I am committed to knowing You, but I do not trust You right now." There were no clapping thunder nor streaks of lightning. It was calm. I could almost hear Jesus saying, "Thank you for being honest. I will make myself known and will win your heart of trust again."

Several more brush strokes had been added to our divine canvas. Christ was now the Jesus of unconditional love, the Jesus of acceptance, the Jesus of grace, and the Jesus of compassion. By promising to love me, He had given me holy permission to be me: fragile, sinful, angry me.

In time, much more paint would be added to the work in progress. The few strokes that were still drying were beautiful, however. It was obvious a portrait was coming together.

# CHAPTER 5

# THE ANNA TRUTHS

*But Mary, the mother of Jesus, kept within herself all these*
*things weighing and pondering them in her heart.*

*Luke 2:19 (AMP)*

Tara's grip nearly caused my pulse to leap out of my hand, not to mention my heart from my chest. She let out a scream of pain and grief as she pushed her long awaited bundle of innocence into the world: screaming lungs, a healthy baby boy, what every mother longs for. This was the pinnacle of peace, the moment of relief, and the permanence of joy every mother knows is hers; however, this would not be the case for Tara. Instead, a countdown had begun. Mother and son both stopped wailing the moment their eyes locked, making their silent declaration to the world: they were in love. The doctor, the nurses, and I watched in grateful agony as this little man tightly grasped his mother's finger. He had no idea it was to be the last time he would share her affection. Two days later, Tara left the hospital with empty hands. She headed back to an apartment barely furnished, cabinets sparse, to her two pleading children and a useless boyfriend.

I needed the adoption to take place fast. I was left in an unbelievable state of shock and pain at what had just taken place. This was my first adoption. Had we really let Tara leave the hospital without him? How could she ever climb out from under the weight of such pain and grief? I had seen the look, heard the cries, and understood the bitterness of her tears as she wept. What had I been thinking in counseling and supporting her in a decision that could cause her such suffering? Without the other piece of the adoption puzzle in play, I was in a clouded state of confusion as to why I had signed up to be a birth-parent counselor.

Later, as I watched precious, handsome, baby James delivered into the aching arms of his new mother, I quickly remembered why I had taken the job. I almost felt like an intruder as he gazed into his adopted mother's adoring eyes. It was a holy exchange. James would grow up with all the affection, tenderness, and support he would ever need. He was loved first by his biological mother. An unsung hero, she is all too often forgotten, my brave friend and mentor in the sacrificial art of true love.

I sat in the waiting room of the counselor's office for the third time, staring once again at the paintings of Jesus hanging on the wall. I wondered what words would come out of my mouth. Pain sloshed against the walls of my heart and mind as I sat much like Tara, arms empty, a mother unable to be a mother. I was a birth mother and nothing more.

As Anna had taken her early flight into God's family way before I ever dreamed possible, I related to the birth mothers who allowed me to hold their hands in labor and in grief. I wanted Anna, but I couldn't keep her. I longed to know if she knew me and loved me and what would become of our relationship that I had so carefully nurtured. Was it over? Did I have no connection to her? When I entered heaven myself one day, would she say, "Who's that lady?" or would she run into my arms crying out "Mama, Mama," as if she'd just been away at a slumber party for the night? As with so many of my clients, I was forced by my circumstances to give her up. Jesus was her new permanent parent. Proclamations from well-meaning saints sitting high up on their holy horses were leading me to believe I should feel relieved that she wouldn't have to grow up in a world full of suffering and sin. I was trying to cling to a God I thought I knew, all the while being pulled and torn away by the clashing and tumultuous winds of irony and agony, a cyclone of suffering.

I felt horribly misunderstood by people who didn't see the connection I had built with her. "How can you miss someone you don't know?" They didn't get it. They didn't understand that I had loved and nurtured her spirit and her body for those nine glorious months. They didn't understand that for months and even years before that, I had prayed and ached for her. One dear friend said that I'd had a pregnant heart for as long as she had known me.

The physicality of "us" was lost, but what about the *spirituality* of "us"? The burning question of my soul was, "Do I still have a relationship with Anna?" It may seem odd, but in spite of the fact that I wasn't looking into her eyes, I had already experienced such an authentic and special relationship with her. Was it still possible? I could deal with not having her physically, but abandoning my spiritual ties to her was too much to bear. As I expressed all of this to my counselor, he encouraged me to ask God to speak to my question about the "us" I was hoping still existed. His answer opened to me the first of many "Anna truths."

## The Golden Scepter

I bowed my head to pray, and as soon as the burning question of "us" passed through my lips, the image was before me.

I stood outside in an unknown spot, as if waiting. Without notice, a single, furious gust of wind raced past my body, snatched Anna from within my womb, and hurled her into the sky. I saw Jesus standing in heaven waiting for the catch. He pulled her to His chest, and I stood alone, weeping uncontrollably. Hanging from me, limp and lifeless, was the umbilical cord. Our physical connection had been severed.

Then I saw myself standing in heaven, and I knew Anna was standing beside me. She appeared to be two or three. We both faced forward, and I knew we were waiting for Jesus to appear. And then there He was, facing us, His reassuring smile emanating hope. His arms were extended out toward us, and across them lay the umbilical cord we had shared, the former sign that we belonged to each other. My eyes focused on Christ's, and He was smiling at me as if he knew something I didn't. I looked back at the cord, and everything had changed. Full of strength and pulsing with vigor, it was alive. Now it lay across His arms as a beautiful rod of glowing splendor, and as He tipped it to me He said, "This is your golden scepter." He stepped forward and placed the scepter between Anna and me. Like Cinderella's glass slipper, it was a perfect fit. Then He extended His hands, exposing His wrists, and silently directed me to view His scars. He touched Anna's belly button and said to me firmly, yet tenderly, as if it were extremely important that I understand, "She bears your mark."

And that was it. I opened my eyes in total bewilderment and astonishment. It was a riddle, and I didn't understand any of it. I had no idea what a golden scepter was, and I was floored that Jesus would entertain and entrust me with such a perplexity of images to explore.

I felt nervous at the thought of verbalizing what I had just envisioned. It seemed more like a crazy dream than a message from Jesus. Nonetheless, it had most certainly come from God. How in the world would I put this into words, and what would the counselor say? He didn't try to make sense of it. He simply encouraged me to go home, seek it out, and allow the Holy Spirit to minister meaning to my mind.

For the rest of the evening and into the night I pondered, prayed, and researched to understand the meaning of the vision. As I wrote on a few sheets of paper, revelation and realization flooded my mind, and the fresh truth of Jesus (or the "true truths" as my mother calls them) came to life.

I found myself studying, eyes and heart wide open to the book of Esther, pages I honestly had never read before. Let me paraphrase:

Queen Esther bravely approached her husband, King Xerxes, with an urgent request. Now to approach the King without invitation was a mighty faux-pas, a royal "no-no." The penalty of such blatant disrespect for the king and his rules was death. So for Esther to take the risk of appearing before her powerful husband without a summons was like voluntarily walking the treacherous steps to the guillotine. Esther was brave, however, and her request was of crucial importance to the life of Mordecai, the Jewish uncle who had raised her. Esther had learned from Mordecai that a decree had been issued for the destruction of his life and his people, the Jews, by order of Haman, the King's right-hand man. Esther was afraid to approach her mighty husband whom she hadn't seen in over a month. But when Mordacai exhorted her, *You were born for such a time as this*, he roused the necessary faith and courage in his niece the queen. Up until this time, her true identity had been carefully hidden. After several days of fasting and prayer to the God of the Jews, Esther put on her best dress and headed for the court of the King's chamber. Would he send her to be hanged for her bold behavior, or would he be won over by her beauty and his love for her? One kingly gesture was all she needed to know her fate.

> *And when the King saw Esther the queen standing in the court, she obtained favor in his sight and he held out to her the golden scepter that was in his hand. So Esther drew near and touched the tip of the scepter. Then the King said to her, 'what will you have Queen Esther? What is your request?' It shall be given to you, even to half of the kingdom (Esther 5:2-3).*

It seemed as though Esther possessed the key to the king's powerful heart, for he was putty in her hands. He had tipped the golden scepter, the rod by which he ruled, the object of his majesty, power, and authority. The tipping of the scepter was a wordless decree, a royal "Yes!" Her request was granted before it was even revealed; life for Esther, life for Mordecai, life for their people (the Jews) was guaranteed.

I was stunned at this story I was hearing for the first time. God was clearly directing me to Esther's life to adopt certain truths for myself. Now I stood before my King waiting, just as Esther had waited for the answer to her request. For Esther, the tipping of the scepter replaced fear with favor and death with life. My request was a connection to Anna, to know that the spiritual ties we shared, independent of heartbeats, breathing, and blood, had been preserved. Jesus took our lifeless physical connection made of human, temporary fabric and replaced it with a bond made of heavenly, royal material. "Jesus, do I still have a connection to my baby girl?" With one tip of the scepter, the answer was a resounding and glorious "YES!"

## THE MARK

*Jesus came and stood among them and said, 'Peace be with you,' He showed them His hands and His side... 'Put your finger here; see My hands... stop doubting and believe' (John 20:19, 27).*

When Jesus appeared to His disciples in the upper room just days after His resurrection, He showed them His scars. It was the moment they believed He was their Jesus, the long awaited Messiah. Just as He had centuries before, Jesus pulled up the sleeves of His robe to direct me to see His scars. Why? He then pointed to Anna's belly button and said, "She bears your mark." Both Anna and Jesus had scars. His scar revealed His relationship to His children as their Savior from sin. Her scar revealed her identity as the daughter of Kate Kelty. I had always thought it was interesting that Jesus bore His scars even in His resurrected body. The scars tell an essential story; they identify suffering, and they prove that He is who He says He is.

The word "mark" is defined as a "distinguishing trait or quality, a symbol used for identification or indication of ownership."[2] I asked, "Jesus, will Anna know who I am? When I enter the kingdom, will she know I am her adoring mother?" My Savior seems to answer, "Yes, for she bears your mark, the

---

[2] Merriam Webster Online Dictionary. 2009. Merriam-Webster Online: 27 April 2009,http://www.merriam-webster.com/dictionary/mark.

mark which is the distinguishing trait of your relationship, the identification of your mother/daughter bond."

> *Yes, if you cry out for insight and raise your voice for understanding. If you seek wisdom as for silver and search for skillful and godly wisdom as for treasures, then you will understand the reverent and worshipful fear of the Lord and find the knowledge of our omniscient God (Proverbs 2: 3-5 AMP).*

I had certainly been crying out for wisdom, and I desperately wanted to know the truth. God could have simply stated the facts instead of sending me a colorful vision to investigate. I believe God was teaching me to hunt for truth like treasure.

That week was an enormous milestone in my grieving journey. There was less to fear with the truth of forever and the knowledge of our permanent bond intact. I was also impressed by God's kindness to speak to me in a way that would inspire me to want to know Him more. I was learning that He could speak to me in unique ways that would blossom into meaning as I searched for understanding. This made the truth that much sweeter when I finally comprehended it. I also believe God was unfolding His truth in such a way that there could be no mistake that it had come from Him. I was asking God bold questions, and He was giving me clear answers. I had not realized that was actually possible. God was speaking to me.

## THE HIDDEN MESSAGE OF THE SCEPTER

When death was plotted against Esther's family, she was called from the shadows and elevated from among many queens. God had carefully hidden her identity in order that she might be His agent of mercy among the Jews. Receiving the extended scepter defined the moment she stepped out onto center stage and into the spotlight to be that which God had created her to be. She truly had been born for such a time as this.

In my weak and fragile state just a few months after the loss of Anna, God reassured me through the life of Esther and through the message of the scepter that our relationship was being preserved. I had no idea that an additional and even more powerful message remained. God was slowly writing a story into my life about the relationship between Jesus and the suffering child. Just as the extension of the scepter to Esther signaled that she would be God's instrument to save the lives of many, I believe in accepting God's scepter that Anna and I will offer life, truth, and healing to the grieving souls of many. I painfully and yet passionately proclaim, "I too was born for such a time as this."

The vision of the scepter was a precious gift from the creative and powerful heart of God tailored just for me. He massaged His truth like healing ointment into the deep wound that remained. Though I still felt angry and astonished at God, there was no denying it: His truth was saving me. Peace was working its way into the enormity of my pain. One day at a time, one truth at a time…Anna was alive, and our relationship was far from over.

# CHAPTER 6

# NURTURING ANGELS

*Praise the Lord, you His angels, you mighty ones who do His bidding, who obey his word. Praise the Lord all His heavenly hosts, you His servants who do His will.*

*Psalm 103:20-21*

As it is for many adolescents, high school was a painful time for me. I was awkward, unsure of myself, and straddling the fence of religion and rebellion. Each day I walked into school just hoping to blend in, dodging the bullets of all the right, but oh-so-wrong people. I wasn't very successful. Life at Harrisonburg High was excruciating until my senior year when God provided me the best friend I'd prayed for in Ruthie. She truly rescued me. But sixteen brought new meaning to the word "misery." Every morning I sought to wrestle the parental reins from my mother, reasoning that staying home was a much better alternative than having to endure the social pain of my peers. I managed to escape six weeks of school over the period of that year. I was later told that the school had adopted a new attendance policy because of me.

One of the days I did manage to get to school was particularly difficult. I can't remember now the exact circumstances, but I sought refuge in a hidden stairwell away from those who mocked me. As I began anxiously walking up the steps, I paused for a brief moment to offer a desperate prayer, "Jesus, help me!" Without a moment's delay, two angels appeared above me in the stairwell. It was as if my mind had projected a scene onto the wall in front of me, revealing a snapshot of the unseen realm. Peace settled over me as I reached the top of the stairs. Completely unafraid, I opened the doorway to re-enter my adolescent nightmare. Though the vision had vanished, I walked down the once treacherous hallway with my head now held high, certain that I was not alone. Even though I had never really heard anything about angels, I had no trouble at all believing that what I had seen in my mind's eye was real. Responding to a simple expression of need, Jesus answered my prayer with an invasion of angels, the *servants that do his bidding (Psalm 103:20)*. As I walked down the crowded hall, a tiny curve found its way to my lips. I knew a secret.

This memory had long been stored in the recesses of my mind until recently when I was preparing to write this chapter and remembered that I had first encountered angels long ago.

When I learned I was pregnant with Anna, my loving friend and mentor Janet told me a story about her daughter that in many ways set the spiritual pace of my pregnancy. One afternoon as Janet's daughter, Tiffany, was rocking her baby to sleep, filling the nursery with her songs of praise, out of the corner of her eye she saw an angel, hand raised, worshipping God. When she turned to look, there was nothing. But as she turned back again, she saw him in her peripheral vision worshipping there. I was overwhelmed by the sweetness of the story, and in that moment, the prayer that my baby's nursery would be a sanctuary was born in me. I don't know if I actually believed God would answer that prayer, or if I just thought it seemed like a beautiful thing to pray, but God did not withhold the answer from me.

It wasn't until after the pregnancy was over and Anna was delivered and relinquished that God would take me back in time and open my eyes to the angel He had placed in our life.

## LULLABY ANGEL

I sank into the rocking chair accompanied by a wave of sobs and closed my eyes seeking to remember the days not long prior when Anna had been inside me, full of life. I settled into a collection of delightful rocking chair memories and was caught off guard when never-before-seen images appeared. As if watching a home video of my recent past, I became aware of details that had been hidden from me before.

> My sacred nook in the corner of the nursery was enveloped by a tent. I saw myself inside, oblivious to the covering, rocking, full of joy and full of baby. Over and over I caressed my stomach joyfully as I sang to Anna…"Baby girl, baby girl, can you see…"

> All of a sudden the scene shifted, and now I sat there weeping. I was still pregnant, but as I clutched my stomach, rocking in desperation, it was obvious I was reliving the last hours I would ever be in this carefully crafted nursery with my sweet girl. As I painfully looked into the memory, I realized that the tent that had previously appeared in the same nook was now gone. Just as I began to wonder why it had disappeared or what its significance had been, I found myself staring at an angel. She was standing by the door, across from me, as if preparing to leave. My Anna Rose rested in the crook of her arms, and I watched as the angel sweetly gazed upon her and softly hummed my song…and on I wept.

When I emerged from the nursery later that day, I felt like I was re-entering earth having been in another world. All I knew at the time was that in my darkest hour, as I ached for the life of my child, simultaneously and unbeknownst to me, an appointed angel was taking her turn as Anna's interim caretaker.

A month later I was forced to wake up and live through my first Mother's Day. The day felt so wrong and so right all at the same time. Part of me wanted to hold a press conference to proclaim that I was still a mother and that this day thus still belonged to me. Yet the other part of me wanted to crawl into a hole and disappear as the world applauded beautiful mothers holding their beautiful babies.

As the day finally came to a close, I took my place for the evening ritual and rocked yet again. With Anna's parcel of ashes pressed as close to my heart as I could get them, I sang, "Baby girl, baby girl can you see…the Father's love is pouring down on thee." And as I closed my eyes to settle into the moment, before me once again was the angel, and then I heard, "Baby girl, baby girl, can you hear…rushing waters, angels everywhere." There she was, infant Anna, snuggled in holy arms, rocking back and forth. It was as if I'd been transported to heaven to peer into a window beholding the precious scene of my baby continuing life in a perfect realm, in a similar fashion to how she had known life with me. Of course I am sure there is much more to her heavenly life than swaying in song, but for some reason, God wanted to extend this beautiful picture to me.

"Happy Mother's Day," He seemed to proclaim as He opened my eyes and gave me the gift of knowing my lullaby continues within the walls of heaven. My mothering is being honored in eternity. My daughter's heart and mind are continually washed in the words and tune her mother wrote just for her.

Last year I came across Psalm 34:7, and I quickly fit together puzzle pieces that had long since been scattered across the floor of my mind. *The angel of the Lord encamps around those that fear him and He delivers them (Psalm 34:7).*

"Encamps," I pondered. Instantly I saw myself tucked away in the nursery, within the tent in the corner of the room, just as my earlier vision had revealed. The tent that had enveloped me during the brighter days of my pregnancy was in fact the symbolic image of the angel of the Lord. "I was encamped within His presence," I thought. I contemplated that realization for another moment, and then as if hit by a lightning bolt of truth in my heart, I finally got it. I laughed out loud. "*She* was encamped within His presence!" I finally understood. This angel was about Anna, not me. It now made sense that the tent had disappeared upon Anna's death, for the angel simply followed the one he was assigned to care for. The verse says that the "angel of the lord *delivers* them." It was true; the angel *had* delivered her spirit from within me as I sat weeping, clutching my belly in the nursery, and soon he would be delivering her to Jesus.

From the moment of Anna's conception, throughout my pregnancy, and in the moment her heart stopped beating, her eyes forever closing, God loved her and was with her. He had not abandoned her. He called her into being, he whispered her name when she was being woven together in the *secret place* (Psalm 139), and I believe she recognized His voice when he called her name upon the threshold of heaven. Somehow the presence of the angel reassured me that she had never been alone. In the hours when I had just assumed her stillness meant she was sleeping, the angel had rocked and sung to her, even in the moments when I had been oblivious to her departure. Hugged by me and then without a moment's lapse in time, she was within God's ministering arms. Yes, God's presence had been with me, but He had also been uniquely, individually, and intimately involved in every second of the life of Anna Kelty. She was also *His* kind of gal. For the first time ever, I began to see Anna not simply as an extension of myself, but also as an individual for whom God cared deeply, completely apart from me. She was my baby, but more than that, she was God's creation. He hadn't just swept in at the last second and taken over. He had been with her all along.

## WORSHIPING ANGEL

There is one final angel vision that God extended during those first desperate months.

> I had lay down to take a nap, and when I shut my eyes, Jesus stood before me. He was standing with His feet shoulder-width apart. His arms extended high above His head, and He held a red sphere in His hands. An angel hovered above Him and poured water onto the sphere with a watering can. Jesus looked at me and said, "It is high and lifted up."

Not long after that, I came across this scripture:

> *I saw the Lord sitting on a throne, high and lifted up, and the train of His robe filled the temple. Above Him stood the seraphim…and one cried to another, holy, holy, holy is the Lord of hosts; the whole earth is full of His glory (Isaiah 6:1-3 NKJ).*

"High and lifted up" is a description of Jesus in the throne room of heaven where angels hover to praise Him. I believe Jesus wanted to reinforce the truth that Anna resided with Him, that she was being held and preserved in His very hands, and that He had appointed His angels to care for her by doing what they do best, worship. Wasn't that always our hope and prayer for her, that she would be a child of worship? And so it continues, forever.

*See that you do not look down on one of these little ones. For I tell you, that their angels in heaven always see the face of My Father in heaven (Matthew 18:10).*

What a powerful and beautiful proclamation from Jesus, exemplified here as the protective father. "Hey listen," He seems to say, "there are invisible body guards for children – called angels – and their job is to watch and wait. They behold the faces of their little ones, and at God's command, they are by their side faster than the speed of light."

I wonder, was that what it had been like at sixteen when I had hidden in the stairwell? Had my angels seen my pain and my anguish? Had they simply waited for Jesus to say the word so they could come to my side? And how had it been for Anna? Had her angel beheld her little face when its muscles flexed for the last time? Had Jesus signaled, "Go" with a look of authority and compassion? Had the angel scooped up her spirit and begun singing as she opened her eyes to her eternal destiny? Had Anna thought at first that she was finally, after all those months, beholding me? Had the angel explained and said, "Welcome sweet little Anna; I am taking you to Jesus."

Sadly enough, even these beautiful revelations of God's nurturing angels didn't erase my accusations and distrust of Him. For three more years I would continue to wrestle with the sovereign mystery of His seemingly cruel hand. Yes, He had given an angel, but He had withheld His power from Anna when all she needed was a simple command to maintain the rhythmic gesture of her heart.

There were still a thousand lies I believed about God, and a million truths to be absorbed. But a picture was slowly developing in my mind and in my heart. Anna's place in heaven was being formed. Certain anxieties and worries were alleviated as I met the nurturers who were filling my shoes until I would arrive to once again sing to my baby girl.

# CHAPTER 7

# THE BEARER

*Then you shall know the truth and the truth will set you free.*

*John 8:32*

*Come to me all you who are weary and burdened and I will give you rest. Take my yoke upon you and learn from me, for I am gentle and humble in heart and you will find rest for your souls. For my yoke is easy and my burden is light.*

*Matthew 11:28-30*

The days rolled on. Every night I sat in Anna's nursery and rocked as I cradled the small box of ashes in my arms. I had wrapped the box in a pale green gown with a mama and baby giraffe kissing on the front. It was a gown Chris had picked out and laid in her empty crib the day before Anna should've arrived, March 17 – St. Patrick's Day. We had joked that Anna was destined for a March 17th birthday because Chris, who is a red-head, is very proud of his Irish heritage. The holiday was now darkened with loss, and Chris walked out of the nursery tearfully proclaiming, "I would've dressed her in this today." And so, of course, that became the swaddling garment. At other times I carefully unfolded the cherished pink-flowered sleeper she had worn in the hospital, her "coming home outfit," and rested it upon my shoulder as if she were nuzzled there as well. I gently traced the stains of blood, precious DNA, symbols that a person – *my person* – had once been bundled inside.

Rocking, I would sing…

"Baby girl, baby girl, can you see? The Father's love is pouring down on thee. Baby girl, baby girl, can you hear? Rushing waters, angels everywhere. You were created in His image, knitted in my womb; with His finger He'll touch that smile upon your face. Baby girl, baby girl can you feel? The hug of heaven, my womb around my shape."

Sometimes it sounded beautiful. I sang with every ounce of love, strength, and pride I possessed. At other times, I whispered, warding off the eruptive floodgates of sorrow crashing against my vocal cords. As time went on, there were days when the well seemed dry, as if I had cried every tear in the reserve. But I forced it anyway. Every night I sat in Anna's room and looked through her photo album, ten rolls of film portraying the eleven hours of her earthly existence, until the escalating wave of grief hit and washed me limp into my bed to recoup for the night. Grief is grueling.

Sweet Chris would come into Anna's nursery and practically carry me into our bedroom. We grieved so differently, yet we had such grace for each other. Tenderness and acceptance wove a banner over our relationship, and we effortlessly (*supernaturally*) met each other's needs. The only thing worse than my own suffering was watching Chris suffer, and so it was for him.

One night Chris said, "Sweets, don't look through her pictures, not tonight." Without hesitating, I defensively responded, "I have to, I haven't cried today." It was that comment and the conversation that followed that showed me I believed shedding my sorrow was keeping my love for her alive. I felt so guilty when I wasn't sad. I was afraid of what it might mean if I weren't expressing my sorrow. So it had become an evening ritual. I made sure that I could go to bed with a clear conscience. After purging the tears, my weary soul would declare, "Yes, today ended bitter. Today ended in grief. Today is a day I loved Anna well."

It was time – time to gather the necessary courage to deal with the enormity of my grief. Now, with Jesus as my ever-present, loving, and gracious Savior, I was ready to step onto the shaky, swinging bridge of suffering. It was time to deal with the excruciating sadness that came from simply uttering her name.

There were two barricades that barred my heart and falsely promised protection from pain. I would soon discover these obstructions to be lies keeping me from true and productive grieving, and from Jesus.

The first barrier was the guilt I suffered for bearing the responsibility of Anna's death. "Was it my fault? Could I have stopped it? I am a failure as a mother!" These sentences berated my heart and mind without ceasing.

The second barrier was the daily routine of grief I was inflicting upon myself. I believed it to be essential to maintaining and growing my love for Anna and equated the degree of my pain with the depth of my love. Jesus was ready and willing to remove each barricade and to enter my heart Himself, to heal me and set me free. But the lies assured me that to let Jesus enter my heart would only take me down a dark road with no way out. Hadn't I learned that trusting God would only hurt me? The enemy constantly reminded me of this lie to keep me from Jesus and to keep my heart barred from His healing presence. Up until this point, Jesus had been reminding me who He truly was. But to ask Jesus to become involved in my pain would require that I be a participant in the relationship that I had deliberately put on hold.

I described my pain to the counselor, unaware that lies had erected themselves like guards at the threshold of my heart. He reiterated to me a lesson in Christ's character and the foundation of his counseling ministry. He explained that it's not just what happens in life that shapes us, but it is also the meaning we give the experience. He further explained that we often come to believe certain things about God that are not consistent with His truth. This results in lie-based pain. The promise here is that for pain derived from the enemy's lies, Jesus is the bearer of truth. He makes an exchange with the enemy's deceit, which will always bring freedom and peace. As promised, *you shall know the truth and the truth shall make you free (John 8:32).*

He also explained that in some sense we are all strugglers, having faced real or perceived losses, resulting in sadness, disappointment, sorrow, and grief – or true-based pain, as he calls it. For this type of pain, Jesus is the burden-bearer. He pleads with us and promises, *Come to me all who are weary and burdened and I will give you rest. Take my yoke upon you which is easy and light and you will find rest for your souls. (Matthew 11:28-30).*

Newly inspired by the truths of God as my burden-bearer and bearer of truth, I was ready to face my pain.

## THE BEARER OF TRUTH

I listened intently at the words the counselor chose to speak to Jesus on my behalf. The previous nervousness I had in wondering if Jesus would appear had now vanished. My heart began to race as I took one last deep breath before stepping through the door of my mind to see Him. Eyes closed, I was simply in His presence. I opened my grieving, guilty heart and verbalized my fear for the impending responsibility of Anna's life. It was time to listen to Jesus and to hear what He thought about me, to hear the truth, no matter how painful and reproving it would be. But the next five words I heard invited me into freedom and joy, not condemnation. I simply heard Jesus say, "You are a holy mother." It was a few moments before I could share the declaration that I'd heard. *Maybe I didn't hear him correctly*, I thought. But then I heard the pronouncement again, peace trailing after, and I knew Jesus was speaking directly to me. As I timidly spoke the statement out loud, my counselor smiled, like a proud father.

Holy means "to the service or worship of God; hallowed; sacred; reserved from common use, holy vessels; holy priesthood."[3] A second definition is "spiritually whole or sound; of unimpaired innocence and virtue, free from sinful affections, pure in heart, Godly, pious, irreproachable, guiltless, acceptable to God."

Can you see me sitting terrified and ashamed, full of guilt on the witness stand with Satan as the examining, accusing attorney, hurling insults and accusations my way?

> "Isn't it true, Kate, that you are responsible for the death of your daughter? You and you alone! Isn't it true, Kate, that you failed her as a mother and that you should therefore spend the rest of your life wrestling with the blame and guilt of such careless, unloving actions?"

> With head bowed low and no energy left to fight, I concede the arguments and buy into every lie. "He is right," I utter in a deep and grievous whisper.

> Then, Jesus rises and in one loud, clear, and silencing statement, He assumes the role of defense attorney,

---

[3] Merriam-Webster Online Dictionary. 2009. Merriam-Webster Online: 27 April 2009, http://www.merriam-webster.com/dictionary/holy.

jury, and judge. "She *is* a holy mother!" I look up, eyes wide with disbelief, yet a flicker of hope. "You are no longer on trial, daughter. You may step down from the witness stand. This woman is spiritually whole. She has unimpaired innocence and virtue. She is free from any sinful affection you accuse her of, Satan, for she is pure in heart, godly, irreproachable, and guiltless. She is more than acceptable to Me and to My Father. She was a holy vessel of My love to her baby. I set her apart, and she worshipped Me as an adoring and godly caretaker of the child I entrusted to her. Kate, you are free...you are a holy mother!"

As I step down from the witness stand, the hand of Christ extended to me, I place a dark parcel in His hand. It is a black box holding the lies for which I had been accused. Jesus takes it from me, and into my hands places a white gift, practically glowing. It is truth. I was a holy mother to my baby girl. With this exchange, I am free. No longer does needless guilt weigh my soul down and stand guard at the gate of my heart. I am free. I am a holy mother.

That day Jesus taught me the power of a lie and the greater power of a truth. He taught me as He once revealed through Paul the importance of *demolishing arguments and every pretension that sets itself up against the knowledge of God, and to take captive every thought to make it obedient to Christ. (2nd Corinthians 10:5).* Jesus was saying, lasso every untrue, deceitful thought that comes your way and present it to the Lordship of Jesus, God of truth, and you will go free.

With one divine declaration, I began to believe the truth and to extol myself as the mother I had always longed to be. And Jesus, this one I had accused, was now my Bearer of Truth.

## THE BURDEN-BEARER

There were but a few minutes left in the one-hour session. After we discussed what had taken place and the power of truth, *that it is for freedom that Christ has set us free (John 8:32)*, we prayed one last time. We beseeched God as the truth-giver, and I clearly understood that one lie remained, the final barricade to my heart. I had to release the lie that pain was the only way to assure myself that I loved Anna. Exhausting myself in the brutal exercises of suffering made me feel like a good and loving mother. Jesus had shown me that this was an unnecessary ritual that was forcing me into a life of misery. In the many moments everyday when the tears and sadness flowed free, I felt guilty for wanting to feel any other way. It seemed that this was simply the way I would have to feel. What would it say about me if I asked Jesus to replace my pain with His peace? Did that mean I wasn't a strong enough mother to handle the pain that such a love would invoke?

My counselor explained that I had a decision to make. It was up to me whether or not I would choose to give these lies to Jesus and ask Him to bear the burden of my grief and sadness. I was so nervous. I didn't want to ask Him to take the pain. I was too afraid that my love for Anna would disappear in the asking. "I'm not ready to do it" I said. I was also afraid that releasing the pain would mean I would never be able to feel sad again. Didn't she deserve that, my sadness for a lifetime? Thinking about parting with sadness seemed inconceivable. I knew the truth—that the grief wasn't the preserving agent of my love for her—but I wasn't ready to part with the lie. It had become for me a warm coat in the midst of a bitter winter. So I left that day with one barricade down, one remaining.

The next couple of weeks were difficult. I felt panicked. There were days when grieving was effortless and necessary. At other moments, I was a willing hostage to the lies that dragged me down into a dark sea of sadness to drown in sorrow. I knew the answer was Jesus, but I continued to turn away from His tender voice, *Come to me, Kate; your soul is so weary and needs the rest I can give. Let's make a trade: your heavy burden for Mine, which is easy and light. Come to me, Kate (Matthew 11:28-30).*

We moved from our house into my sister's home. She and her family moved to Colorado, yet another loss in our life. It was a tremendous gift as well. Our house was so small and dark, and every inch of it whispered Anna's name. Kristen and Mike's house was large and bright and turned the page to a new chapter that was so desperately needed. Unable to take down Anna's nursery, I set it up once again in the exact same way in what had been my niece Beth's nursery.

One particular afternoon I was overcome with sorrow, and the panic set in. The house was quiet. Chris was gone. I was unable to think of anything else and began to relive every shocking and tragic moment of the loss. I sat in Anna's new nursery, and I began to hyperventilate. Chris typically held my hand through these moments and helped me breathe and calm down. Now I was alone. I was afraid for myself. The words of King David reverberated through my anguish: *the cords of death entangled me, the anguish of the grave came upon me; I was overcome by trouble and sorrow. Then I called on the name of the Lord; Oh Lord save me (Psalm 116: 3-4).* With no one else to turn to, I desperately cried out to Jesus.

"Jesus, save me! Jesus, I can't do this anymore. I can't feel this way anymore. I want to die. Jesus I want you to take the pain, but I am so afraid of what will happen if you do. Jesus… Jesus, I need you!"

I could no longer maintain the grieving and the oppression of Satan's lies. As soon as the name of Jesus passed my lips and my feeble hands reached out for help, He was there.

> Inches from my face, Jesus peered into my eyes. His hands firmly pressed against my cheeks as He tenderly proclaimed, "Sweetie, I will take the pain, not the love." And with that said, the pain and the panic of that moment were gone.

> I sat as a little girl on the floor and continued to watch Jesus gaze into my eyes with the same loving kindness that had greeted me in our very first encounter in that first counseling session. He kept one hand on my face, and with the other hand, He stroked my hair. For that moment, I was nothing more than a little girl with her daddy.

I felt overcome with indescribable peace and true comfort. In that moment I understood why Peter, James, and John had wanted to build a tent for the Lord at the transfiguration. The moment was so rich with satisfaction; I simply didn't want it to end. And in that moment, somewhere deep within I knew: Jesus was the answer for everything I was created for and the remedy for everything I lacked.

After some time, I reluctantly opened my eyes to find the same nursery of my vision. There was one difference. An air of serenity was in the room, and an even greater atmosphere of love. With the lie removed and the burden of pain lifted, there was now room for truth and its fruit. And for the first time since losing Anna, joy accompanied my love for her. It was circumstantially inexplicable, and yet supernaturally the reality of that moment. It was greater than anything I could've imagined.

I learned that day how to call on Jesus for rescue. The grief wasn't taken away permanently. No, the grief, like the sea, comes in waves, sometimes gentle and sometimes vicious. But each time I call on His name, He speaks to the waves and captures my pain once again with His peace. He lifts the burden and invites me to rest, to find reprieve, and to be restored.

Jesus was so much more than I ever knew. I cherish my husband, but I am so glad he wasn't there that day to hold my hand, or I might not ever have reached out for the help of God. I now knew Jesus more fully than I ever had. He was my burden-bearer, the bearer of truth, and deep within a new revelation was growing: I was created to be satisfied by Him.

CHAPTER 8

# THE GREAT EXCHANGE

*My peace I leave with you; my peace I give to you.*
*I do not give to you as the world gives. Do not let*
*your hearts be troubled and do not be afraid.*

*John 14:27*

*You will keep him in perfect peace whose mind*
*is stayed on you because He trusts in you.*

*Isaiah 26:3*

Everyday I felt lighter as the weight of unnecessary burdens and lies was lifted from my life. It became easier to breathe as I found my way out of entanglement. Recognizing Jesus as my burden-bearer and my bearer of truth meant being able to come expectantly before Him for an exchange any time I discerned it. I would exchange my lies for His truth and my burdens for His freedom. Sometimes I found that where there was a burden, deceit existed right alongside it. For example, the burden of sadness was often met with the lie that I would never be happy again. Or the burden of disappointment was met with the lie that I could never hope again. Lies are mischievous little devils. Like leeches, they feast on suffering. One thing was certain: anytime I was able to identify and give Jesus a lie or a burden, peace was left as a monument in that battlefield. Peace was and is powerful.

*And the **peace** of God which transcends all understanding will **guard** your hearts and minds in Christ Jesus....Let the **peace***

*of Christ **rule** in your heart....The God of **peace** will soon **crush**
Satan under your feet....For He himself is our **peace**, He who
has made the two one and has **destroyed** the barrier. The mind
**controlled** by the Spirit is life and **peace**.*

Peace is a happy little word, isn't it? It conjures up images of
"raindrops on roses and whiskers on kittens"...peaceful thoughts
for the storms in our lives. Can you hear Julie Andrews singing with
the Von Trapp children as she teaches them what many of today's
psychologists teach their clients: the power of positive thinking? I
was learning that true peace was not simply the presence of calm
or the temporary absence of chaos. The bold verbs in the scriptures
above—guard, rule, crush, destroy, and control—convey that peace
is an active, aggressive force for good in one's life. They also reveal
that the true giver of peace is Jesus, not "cream-colored ponies
and crisp apple strudel," not circumstance or conditions. In other
words, lasting soul-peace requires the destruction or removal of
chaos by Him, the embodiment of peace.

Imagine the white flag of surrender from the enemy camp
as the great captain of the army approaches to fight the battle.
With one look at His greatness, the enemy soldiers run for the
flag. They know they can't stand up against this champion. I
was watching my life like a war movie, and every battle where
Jesus appeared was a place where yet another white flag was
lifted high. Jesus simply demands peace in the lives of His
asking children.

Christ victoriously rescued me from many battlefields in my
heart and mind. They were frontline conflicts that surfaced as I
tried to move on with life after loss. For me, some of the greatest
battles came in situations where the lie, "The pain will be too
great," left me paralyzed and unable to take life's next step. I was
in desperate need of a great exchange with the Prince of Peace.

## The Pain of New Babies

Two of my dearest friends, Karla and Raegan, were expecting baby girls at the time of our loss. Emma was due in August, and Mallaney due in September. Little girls, bundles of femininity – how could I possibly endure the pain of it? I don't just mean the pain of watching my friends revel in what I would not experience, but the pain of losing again, losing my friends. How could I go and lay in their laps a blundering of tears as they nursed their babies? It wouldn't be fair, to me or to them. Would this end our friendship? I didn't want to be without them, yet I didn't know how I could go on with them. I had tried my hardest to avoid babies. I didn't let my eyes wander at the grocery store, and I avoided the baby aisles at Target. Life was forcing me into a new chapter I was once again unready to encounter.

Emma was born. I wasn't able to go to the hospital for my friend Karla's delivery. It would have been the first time back since Anna was born, and I knew I wasn't ready to return. A couple of months later, Mallaney was born. Raegan, her mother, was my college roommate, and I was furious that I couldn't be there for her. It was in the middle of the night when I received the phone call that Mallaney had arrived. I heard her healthy cries in the background and Raegan's declaration, "It's a girl, Katie," and I crumbled under the pain. I crawled across the bed into Chris's arms and wept for the rest of the night.

As I sat on the counselor's couch the next day, I cried another thousand tears. If a scab had been forming over the wound, it had just been ripped off. I could barely stand to think of my dear friends nursing and rocking their babies while I sat at home – arms empty, nursery empty, and life empty. I felt facing them now would be a pain too great; it would throw me back into the midst of the storm, and I was determined to avoid that at all costs. Being disengaged was terribly painful as well. I had lost my baby and my friends, and now I was losing the ability to be myself. There was pain in staying away, and even greater pain in going to see them. I was tortured.

I shared with my counselor all that had transpired, and he simply began to pray. With cautious and eager expectation, I closed my eyes to behold the following:

> There were three houses sitting in a row. I recognized them immediately: mine in the middle with each of my friends' on the right and left. The lens of my mind narrowed and placed a single room from each house side by side. I peered through the open windows to behold three mothers in three different nurseries. Each rocked and sang, the two on the ends dressed in elegant, flowing white gowns, nuzzling their infants. I then saw myself in the middle bent over in grief, clutching a small box wrapped in a powder green gown. The contrast between the three women was stark and overwhelming. Then suddenly, Jesus was there. I became acutely aware of His presence to my right as I stood on the sidewalk, desperately wanting to run away. I could almost hear His words, echoing from the pages of scripture, *I am the Lord your God, who takes hold of your right hand and says to you, do not fear, I will help you (Isaiah 41:13).*

> He reached for my hand and led me to Raegan's house. We drew close to the window, and I peered inside, taking in every detail of her perfect life. I knew He wanted me to thoroughly feel the pain. When I was truly in touch

with the sorrow, Jesus looked at me and said, "Now give it to me." I looked down to discover a package in my hands, a parcel of pain. I handed it to Jesus. With a knowing smile, He threw it into the air. The box became a bird, a white dove flying into the heavens. Our eyes locked; He simply said, "Peace!"

Then He walked me to Karla's home. As we approached the nursery window, the same course of events took place. I saw with the eyes of my heart all that was tragically lost in my life and all that my friend was enjoying, and I felt waves of sorrow. Jesus requested the pain, and just as before, I gave it to him. He threw it, and the dove once more disappeared. "Peace," He said.

I opened my eyes and blinked to see clearly. It was the same sensation one has when walking out of a dark movie theatre into the brightness of light. I felt like I had been somewhere else. As I shared the vision with my counselor, I was wonderfully aware of the calm and peace that had settled in my heart. Jesus was my hero and my champion, my Prince of Peace.

Equipped with this fresh sense of peace, I made an official trip to each of my friends' houses a few days later. Nervously, I pulled the car over just short of their homes and settled myself down inside my heart by simply singing, "Baby girl, baby girl can you see…." With the final words sung, I was able to park the car and make the journey up the sidewalk. I wasn't exactly sure what to expect, but I hoped peace would be a part of it. Singing the song was a reminder to my heart and mind that Anna Kelty was the baby I longed for, and no other.

In each instance, I smiled and even laughed as I met these sweet baby girls. My friends were the ones who cried – for me, for Anna, and for the unfairness and the pain of it all. I'm not saying the sadness was gone; rather, God's peace had restrained the pain and enabled me to be present and to endure. The lie was that the pain would be too great. Jesus, the truth-giver, proved to me that it was not. Jesus, my burden-bearer, lifted and carried my sorrow so that my friendships with Karla and Raegan were restored and deepened. In that experience, a monument of peace was built as a testament to God's victory. The vision, now a precious memory, exists in my experiential history with Christ. I draw from this history each time I need a fresh reminder of the supernatural peace only Christ Jesus can give.

Over the next year, I had many opportunities to babysit Mallaney. I remember vividly rocking her and singing to her, amazed that I wasn't tormented by the experience. She had become such a gift to me. Some time later, I made a trip back to Kentucky and visited both Emma and Mallaney. I had the privilege of snuggling and reading to them both, playing with their long hair and admiring their femininity. They were three. Anna would have been three. There was peace. *Now may the Lord of peace Himself give you peace at all times and in every way (2 Thessalonians 3:16).* This promise was proving to be true in my life.

## The Pain of Worship

I will never forget singing my first solo in church at the age of thirteen. It was Christmas Eve, and my voice was soft but bright as I sang, "Lo how a rose e'er blooming, from tender stem hath sprung. Of Jesse's lineage coming, by faithful prophets sung. It came a floweret bright amid the cold of winter, when hath spent was the night"[4] (Based on Isaiah 11:1).

---

4   Baker, Theodore. "Lo How A Rose E'er Blooming" 1894

My precious grandfather was wasting away in a nursing home with Parkinson's disease. My father recorded the song, and we took the cassette to Georgia to play for him. It was his last Christmas. Dementia had set in, and Granddaddy was losing his mind. Abandoning his English, he now spoke frequently in Portuguese. He had been a missionary to Brazil for forty years, and was confused to say the least. He responded very little and was difficult to engage. A fog had settled over his heart and mind, and we were losing him. As we sat at a table in the living room of Bud Terrace in Decatur, Granddaddy sat glassy-eyed and blank as my tune rang in the air. When the song came to an end, my hope that he would be brought back to his senses by once-loved lyrics was dashed. As I stood to walk away in despair, the old man, wrinkled and withered, stared expressionless. Tears dampened his cheeks, disappearing into his white wooly beard. He may have forgotten who I was and where he was, but one thing was clear to me. Granddaddy's spirit, evidenced by his tears, was becoming more and more alive by the hour as his eternal destiny drew near.

I remember singing at his funeral, "Great is thy Faithfulness, Oh God my father" and forcing the words through deep sobs. It was difficult, but I was learning for the first time to cling to worship amidst the pain of grief.

Now, twelve years later, the lesson had seemingly escaped me. Pushing through sorrow for song seemed an unbearable feat. The words of worship and the notes reduced me to a pile on the floor and put me in touch with a pain I didn't feel I could withstand. My most meaningful and memorable moments with Anna were the ones accompanied by song. Experiencing worship without her was excruciating. With the lie, "the pain will be too great," buckled tightly around my heart, I stayed away from worship and the resulting comfort and healing. I'm sure Satan took great delight in every lie I chose to believe. He wanted nothing more than for me to be withheld from God's love and freedom.

For four months I kept worship at bay. I can't think of a single day in my previous life when notes weren't spilling from my mouth. I had built a dam to protect myself, but the rapids of song were growing stronger. Chris and I had gone to Daytona Beach to meet up with my sister's family for a much needed respite. They were on a summer project with Campus Crusade for Christ. Nervously, I accompanied Kristen to a worship service one evening. I stood in the back, afraid of how I might respond. The worship began, songs of God's mercy, His love, His sovereignty, His goodness. The music in me was begging to be released, and the dam was cracking under the weight. I opened my mouth, and a few hoarse notes emerged. I instantly shut down as the tears came. I knew I wasn't ready for this. The pain swelled, and I was afraid of what might become of me.

At the very moment I shut my eyes and winced to restrain my emotions and my tears,

> two little eyes peered into mine, and two delicate hands cupped my wet face. With a voice as tender and sweet as I have ever heard, a little girl said, "Come on mama, you can do it!"

I held my breath. I was overwhelmed. It had come in such a quick flash, but it was my Anna, my baby girl. She was cheering me on. She held my face just as Jesus had in the nursery, reminding me He would "take the pain and not the love." Had she witnessed that encounter? Was she, like all children, imitating her Father?

It was the second time I had stared into her eyes. Just two weeks before we lost her, I gazed at the ultrasound monitor just inches from my face, watching Anna sleep. Free and frequent sonograms were a perk of my working at the Pregnancy Center. During that last sonogram, Anna had suddenly blinked, and with eyes wide open, looked straight ahead as if she were staring straight into my eyes and into my soul. It had taken my breath away.

In my vision of Anna holding my face and encouraging my praise, it became clear that healing and joy were waiting for me on the other side of the tears. I had to release the lie of unbearable pain and accept the truth that Jesus would not only bear the pain for me, but restore me with unimaginable healing as well. Now, I was desperate to sing. I had a direct request from my daughter, and I was aching to fulfill any request she might have for her mama. I opened my mouth and allowed the escalating wave of song to crash at the feet of Jesus. I felt a cascading warmth flood over me, and I knew it was His delight. I pressed on, and I imagined Anna singing the same song. It was a holy moment. I felt that we were together again, the moments of worship so greatly enjoyed when I was full of her, received anew in a spiritual realm I can barely describe.

For, *blessed are those who dwell in your house and in your presence; they will be singing your praises all day long (Psalm 84:4)*. Now the child was teaching the parent what it meant to be "a child of worship."

On what would have been Anna's first birthday, my family traveled to Georgia for the unexpected funeral of my uncle Steve. As I sat in the pew, watching my cousins and my Aunt weeping, the piano began to play "Great is thy Faithfulness." It is our family hymn, sung religiously for years at every gathering. I mentioned earlier that we had sung it at Granddaddy's funeral as well. At Anna's memorial service, I was unable to muster the notes. But now with a new opportunity, on my baby girl's birthday, I reached for my sister's hand and began to sing. Instantly, I saw above me standing in a row, my Granddaddy, Uncle Steve, and Jesus. Anna was on Granddaddy's once feeble shoulders, and together, they sang. They were with us, they were viewing our pain, but for them, there was only joy. In that moment, this scripture came to life for me:

*Therefore since we are surrounded by so great a cloud of witnesses, let us throw aside everything that hinders and the sin that so easily entangles and let us run with perseverance the race marked out for us (Hebrews 12:1 AMP).*

At a worship service four months after I had lost Anna, and again months later at my Uncle Steve's funeral, I saw the cloud of witnesses. I sensed the faces of my family – the appointed saints who were cheering us on from the stands of heaven. This reality, this truth, brought greater freedom, and I longed to throw aside the hindrances, to heed their heavenly cheering, and to run the race marked out for me.

I was learning that as I moved forward with my life, I would consistently be confronted with the same decision: press through the pain with the Prince of Peace by my side or remain stuck, surrendering to the lies of the enemy. In these recorded instances of pain, I chose to move forward. I chose to experience the Prince of Peace, and in choosing Him, I chose Jesus.

# CHAPTER 9

# FORGIVENESS DAY

*Bear with each other and forgive whatever grievances you may have against one another. Forgive as the Lord forgave you.*

*Colossians 3:13*

Unfortunately, people don't come with crisis manuals. I remember thinking how unfair it was that in addition to the pain of loss, hurt feelings were sprinkled on top like a bitter garnish to a bitter meal. We were hurt by beloved friends and even family, however well-intentioned they may have been. People we thought would draw near stayed away. Friends, hurt by our distance, withheld grace during our time of need.

Our humanness prevents us from being able to love perfectly amidst tragedy. We aren't wired that way. We all have different triggers and different needs. We tried to keep a posture of grace, but the hurt pierced through our thin exteriors and found the way to our hearts.

My sister shared with me an image a grieving friend had once shared with her. When the storms of crisis hit and thrust you into the frantic waters, some friends will rise to the surface and tread as long as it takes, while others quickly sink to the bottom. How true this was for us. Some of the people I would have bet on to hang in there disappeared, and others I thought would swim for shore stuck by our side.

God gave me a handful of friends who absolutely sewed their hearts to mine and made the decision to walk the long road of grief with me. They became comfortable with my pain and knew how to offer an "I'm sorry" for the hundredth time and how to "not fix it." They learned when to add their tears to mine and when to be strong. They made themselves students of my pain and allowed the compassion of Jesus to be their guide. Instead of taking offense at my moments of distance, they committed themselves to graciousness. They were and are the most faithful people I know.

Cards and phone calls came our way with words that were intended to comfort but didn't...

"The Lord gives and the Lord takes away, may the name of the Lord be praised! Aren't you blessed that your little girl is in heaven with Jesus and away from any suffering she may have experienced in this world? It's good that God took her when He did, maybe she would have been brain dead and God was protecting you. As soon as you have another baby the pain will go away."

But the most painful words for me were, "I hear you are having a crisis of faith." The question pierced my heart. Admittedly, I was angry at God, but I was clinging to Him and fighting every day to *prevent* a crisis of faith. Every day I begged, "Oh Lord, help me to grieve in a holy way. I pray this would make me better and not bitter." I was wrestling for sure, but I was in the ring! I felt judged and misunderstood.

People asked questions that were actually badly disguised opinions: "Had you feared this would happen?" (as if fear were the cause) or, "I heard a distant relative of yours was stillborn. Did you know this? Did you break the generational curse?"

Our humanity leaves us ill-equipped and uncomfortable with grief. Instead of sitting quietly in the agony of another's pain, we feel the need to pull out our spiritual tool box and fix it. Sadly, these honest efforts can come across as pious judgments and callous instructions.

Grief is lonely. When others who've grieved with you recover from the "shock" of the loss and resume life, they assume you've had sufficient time to do so as well. Compassion takes a backseat as opinions and judgments are tossed about more freely. I remember well the pain of judgment extended from others who disagreed with the way I was managing my life and circumstances. Grace was replaced by certain expectations of my performance. It seemed as though people were waiting for the old me to return, for "getting over it" to bring back the Kate they once knew. They didn't get it. She would never return. I would one day emerge from the rubble, but not the same Kate as before. Death changes everything.

Talking to fellow grievers has made me aware that my experience wasn't unique. Forgiveness became an additional and necessary step to continue healing and freedom. For me there were certain hurts that were simply too excruciating to forgive.

## FORGIVENESS DAY

I sat on the leather couch for yet another week, overcome and overwhelmed. With all the progress made, there was still work to do, much like a Thanksgiving plate that seems to grow instead of shrink. Week after week, I chose other topics to discuss rather than my bruised feelings. I had not realized how toxic a lack of forgiveness could be and how essential it was to my overall healing. I had mentioned these injured relationships and the hurt and anger that had festered there. The therapist wanted to discuss it further and to pray about it, but I was reluctant. I didn't want to forgive. As I shared and prayed with my therapist, it became abundantly clear that I was holding tightly to the lie that to forgive meant I was condoning the hurt. I felt so justified, and the thought of letting go made me feel vulnerable. I had no control over the hurt I felt because of death. I could, however, control my forgiveness. Withholding forgiveness felt like power. I feared letting go would open me to greater abuses. I used resentment as an umbrella to shield me from any further downpours of disappointment. As I vetoed my counselor's suggestion to present my hardness of heart to God, he instead lifted a prayer that we would know what we should deal with that day.

As I closed my eyes to pray…

I was staring directly into the mouth of a tunnel. It was dark and seemed like a concrete channel or a sewer pipeline. I stared into the dark mouth of the hole and sensed it extended for a long distance. I was curious about the image and desperately wanted to know what the Lord was seeking to communicate to me. My eyes crawled the distance, and I began to see the letter S flashing in front of me. I was confused and curious. As I reached the end of the tunnel, the S appeared again, followed by four more letters. "STUCK" was now written across the screen of my mind. I continued to wait, but nothing more came. I opened my eyes to relay the account to the counselor. He asked Jesus to show me what "STUCK" meant.

As I waited and listened, a light suddenly turned on inside the opaque cylinder, and as I looked up, a large anchor hooked the opening. My eyes continued to follow the anchor's rope up and as I looked back, I realized the tunnel was lying on the bottom of the ocean floor. The top of the rope emerged from the water and looped over the side of a large boat. My eyes continued the journey until I was standing on the bow of the boat facing what seemed to be an incredible cargo of wooden crates and boxes. God was sending me on a mission to figure something out. I was eager to solve the mystery.

As I took a closer look at the boxes, each one had a label. In bold letters they were inscribed with the names of people, offenses, and the negative emotions I was battling. Some were definitely larger than others. As I looked over the side of the boat, I saw that it was barely staying afloat. This was my life. I was "STUCK" and couldn't move ahead because un-forgiveness and hurt were weighing me down. At that moment, Jesus appeared to my right and gently encouraged me to give Him the crates. I was reluctant to let go of the hurt I felt so justified in carrying. But in that moment I knew that holding onto the hurt was only hurting me more. I also knew that to forgive would release me from not only the pain, but also from the lie that to forgive would condone the offense. I became aware of my own sinfulness and the grace offered me by Christ. To forgive was not just an act of obedience but an act of gratitude for the forgiveness extended to me, and also an act of worship.

My counselor encouraged me to express the hurt and pain I felt from each situation. And to my surprise, as I came honestly before Jesus, I received His compassion for the very real and valid pain each hurt had caused me. And then, I began to give Him my crates, my boxes of bitterness, and my deepest hurts, and one by one, He took them. He stepped into His boat which was next to mine and began to pile the boxes onto the deck. As I relinquished each box, I felt the weight of my life lift a little, my boat now beginning to float again with greater ease. I was amazed that with all of the heavy cargo now added to His boat, there was no change in its buoyancy. I could feel the Holy Spirit once again writing truth onto the tablet of my heart, *Come to me all who are weary and burdened and I will give rest. Take my yoke upon you, for my burden is easy and light and you will find rest for your weary souls (Matthew 11:29-30).*

I had believed that to forgive would cause more pain, justifying the offender. But in fact, forgiveness, though unnatural, was the supernatural agent that lifted the anchor, sending me on my way once again to discover greater healing.

I was amazed at the innovative way God chose to lead me into freedom. I was unwilling to pursue or even discuss forgiveness. So He took me through a tunnel at the bottom of the ocean to reveal my sin. If Jesus had simply walked up to me and said, "Kate, you are stuck and need to offer forgiveness," I think I would have turned and walked away. I am so grateful the Lord tailored His love and pursued me where I needed His healing most.

One of the questions I had for Jesus was how to love and forgive someone who continues to offend in the same way over and over again. He simply showed me that I just needed to keep handing over the boxes. This lesson in forgiveness is how I most often work toward forgiving now. I literally imagine myself on the boat. I get a big black marker, write out the offense and the name of the offender, honestly express my hurt, allow Jesus to comfort and speak truth where needed, and then hand it to Jesus.

That was an amazing and exhilarating day for me. I was validated and comforted by Jesus due to the sin of others, and then I untangled myself from my own sin. Chris had been saying to me for weeks, "Kate, please don't add unnecessary pain to your grief." I just hadn't known how to let it all go. I had listened to the enemy's whisper and believed him that offering forgiveness was the antithesis of freedom. But once again the truth rescued me from the enemy's grip. I was released from unnecessary additional pain. In extending forgiveness I had pulled up the anchor, making it possible to sail forward. I stood on the bow of the boat, and deep in the distance, I could see both goodness and grief on the horizon.

PART THREE

# PAIN

CHAPTER 10

# JOHN JOHN

*The thief comes only in order to steal, kill and destroy. But I came that they may have and enjoy life, and have it in abundance.*

*John 10:9-10 (AMP)*

Two pink lines. A positive test revealed we were pregnant once again. The due date was February 22, 2006, the same day we had lost Anna the year before. Was it a perfect sign of redemption or a bad omen to be reliving the same dates all over again? The joyous and terrifying news came just three grueling months after our loss. I had been cautioned that to get pregnant too soon could interrupt grieving and make bonding with the new baby difficult. Pregnancy was the only way to get parenthood back, and waiting was simply not an option for us. I wouldn't even entertain it.

I was no longer working at the pregnancy center, having signed on to be a full-time griever. I read, I sang, I prayed, I nurtured the new baby to the best of my ability, and I continued to center my actions and efforts as much as I could on Anna. I still wouldn't allow myself to hang up some of my mothering rituals to her. Looking back now, I know my inability to let go was hurting me, but a complete moving forward was unthinkable at the time. Every night Chris would pray, "Lord show us how to move on with her" as I would pray, "Lord teach me how to be the mother of a heavenly child." We were desperate to hang onto that for which hanging on was acceptable. I wanted to find a loophole in the death system. I wanted to dismiss all of the alleged "good-bye stuff" to be able to thrive in a spiritual connectedness to her. I was her mother, and I planned on thinking of her and dreaming of her and acting toward her with every ounce of energy and passion I could muster.

I was clinging to Jesus, half from a heart of need and the other half from fear. I knew there was a part of me that loved Him deeply. How could I not? He was clearly pursuing me, breaking through my darkness in beautiful, transformative ways. He had become so wonderful, so loving, so saving...or had He? I tried to ignore the accusatory thoughts and feelings that continued to push to the surface. Beautiful truths were blooming after months of barrenness. However, the same prickly lies kept coming back, seeking to choke out the buds of truth that anchored my heart and mind. Some days I was triumphant, while on other days I felt controlled by anger, doubt, and blame.

Four months had passed since that dreadful day. A new season was approaching, and a new prayer petition was being lifted. Journaling has always been, for me, a means of self-discovery in the confusion and chaos of life. After losing Anna, the task seemed too draining at first. Now it seemed necessary. I dug around for the pen and black book I had pushed to the back of the closet....

June 20, 2005

> Almost four months ago we lost Anna, my beautiful little girl, my first baby, my flesh and blood. What a tremendous masterpiece she was. I have been unable to write until now. How do you put love, grief, and pain

into words? It almost seems that in trying to define it, my experience is diminished. Something gets lost in the translation of feelings to vocabulary. Words don't seem adequate to express the magnitude of what I have so painfully and intimately encountered these past few months. There is so much to say, however, so much to document about love, suffering, hope, and pain. Over the past four months, God has truly administered healing salve to this wounded soul. In my strange dance of need and anger at God, I can imagine that if I had a blameless heart, I would surely faint from the constant presence and perfection of God's love and care for me, especially at the moments when I least feel it.

And then there's my love, my love for Anna, which seems to grow stronger and more desperate by the hour, testifying to the truth that love never fails. There have been so many visions, so many pictures of Jesus, of angels, of heaven, and of Anna. Truth has brought a peace and comfort that didn't exist at first. My main battles to fight now are the waves of sadness, the suffering of why, and fear of the future. Speaking of the future...we are pregnant, five weeks along, to be exact. What joy, and yet what fear. Cognitively, I am already impressed and enamored with the wonder of this child, yet I am terrified of loving and losing again. I am so faithfully in love with Anna. I am questioning and pondering the how's of loving another child.

I had gotten to some semblance of being in a good spot with God, and now this new pregnancy has me reeling once again about His character and involvement in my life. Will He be present? Will He intervene? Will He let me raise this baby? Will He answer my prayers? Does He care? How do I trust a God that I struggle to find trustworthy?

One day at a time, one moment at a time, one emotion at a time. This is how I am learning to live.

## A NAME

As scared as we were, we certainly had our own little "A team" in place to fight the battle. Doctors, friends, family, frequent ultrasounds, and other medical interventions made us feel like we would survive and prevail. The ultrasounds gave us snapshots and home videos of the new baby who was very eager to reveal that he was a boy. And I felt disappointed. I wanted another daughter, and I felt horribly guilty and saddened because of my feelings. After experiencing so much grief, I wanted to feel nothing but joy regarding this new life. Why did everything have to be so complicated?

One afternoon I was driving home, and out of desperation I pleaded, "Lord, give me a unique love for this child." The Holy Spirit prompted me with a question: "Ask me for his name." I had prayed fervently for Anna's name, yet it hadn't even occurred to me to pray for a name for our son. So a bit hesitantly, and also excitedly, I prayed, and a name I had not yet considered immediately came to my mind. When I got home that evening I said to Chris, "I prayed today for a name for the baby, and I believe God gave it to me." Before I said the name out loud, in that very moment, the same name occurred to Chris. "John," I said. Chris smiled and responded, "If there is anyone I would want to honor by naming our son after him, it would be your dad."

A few days later, I picked up my favorite book read many times over, <u>Abba's Child</u> by Brennan Manning. As I re-read a favorite section of the book, I put my hand to my heart as its significance suddenly took on a whole new meaning. Here is what Brennan had to say about the beloved disciple:

> "One of his disciples, whom Jesus loved, was reclining on Jesus' bosom" (John 13:23-25 AMP). As John leans back on the breast of Jesus and listens to the heartbeat of the great rabbi, he comes to know Him in a way that surpasses mere cognitive knowledge. John experiences Jesus as the human face of the God who is Love. And in coming to know who Jesus is, John discovers who he is – The disciple Jesus loved."[5]

I'll never forget the first time I read these words. I was in Belarus as a student missionary one summer, and I begged God to let me hear His heartbeat and to know His love. Now the word "heartbeat" filled me with a desperation and hope I had never known it was possible to feel. Not only did I long to feel this child's heart beating against my own, but like never before, I also longed for the intimate and comfortable relationship John had with Jesus: to recline against Him, to hear the rhythm of His love pounding, and to have peace and appreciation without distrust or fear of God. This longing would also become my prayer for our son, that one day he would know himself as the beloved of God.

In preparing for John, I knew I needed to deal with some of the more difficult emotions I had with regard to loving a new baby, particularly a son. Would he love me like I imagined my

---

[5] Brennan Manning, Abba's Child; The Cry of the Heart for Intimate Belonging (Colorado Springs: NavPress, 1994), p124.

daughter would? Would I be able to love him like I loved Anna? I was hoping God would speak to me and give me whatever it was I lacked to navigate mothering a son while still loving my daughter. I scheduled one final counseling session before John's birth. I shared all of my thoughts with my therapist, and in expected fashion, he prayed for God to open my eyes to the truth I needed, and God did:

## WINGS AND COURAGE

> I sat at a kitchen table where I was sewing. A little boy around the age of five stood next to me, watching. I appeared to be sewing a costume for him.

> Again I saw myself sewing. Our project was a pair of wings. This time the boy was older, and he tried on the flight suit I had made. The scene repeated itself a few more times. Each time the wings were fitted and adjusted for the growing boy. Then he put them on for the last time, and he flew off. But just before he disappeared into the distance, he turned, came back, hugged and kissed me, and said, "Mother, I esteem you."

Esteem is, "to be held in especially high regard; to set a high value on and to praise accordingly."[6] Can a mother think of any better compliment or honor than to be esteemed by her son? I was so afraid that a son would mean friendship and mentoring from Chris and just supper and laundry from me. I was now filled with an unleashed desire to raise this young man

---

[6] "esteem." Merriam Webster Online Dictionary. 2009. Merriam-Webster Online: 27 April 2009 <http://www.merriam-webster.com/dictionary/esteem>

who would one day esteem me. I now believed our relationship would be a value to us both.

The wings were also of extreme importance. The job of a mother is never to cling but to prepare her offspring for a day when they will make their leap from the nest. I allowed the vision to speak to my heart about my approach to raising John; however, I was unable to see the truth and direction God was giving me in regard to letting Anna fly. I needed permission to stop working on her wings. She was gone, yet I continued sewing as if it were of great importance to her. It would be another couple of years until I could finally embrace the fact that she no longer needed me, and maybe even more painful to admit, that I no longer needed her. If I stopped "sewing" for Anna, would that mean I didn't love her anymore and didn't recognize her value? I needed to be able to put down my needle and thread to experience all the healing God had for me and to be able to fully focus my attention on my son.

Once again, God spoke to me about letting go. I saw Jesus just as I had in a previous vision:

> His arms were extended above His head, and He held a red sphere in His hands proclaiming, "It is high and lifted up." I knelt on the ground before Jesus with my right arm stretched up high, touching the sphere, my promised relationship to Anna. Jesus stood before me with a sword, and just as a king to a knight, He touched the sword to my right and my left shoulder, then to the top of my head, and spoke these words: "I crown you with courage."

The courage with which God christened me wasn't just the courage this new pregnancy required. He was knighting me with the courage to remove my hand from the sphere, enabling me to step away from the relationship which was being preserved for the appointed time. It needed no tending from me. It was "high and lifted up" and could not be harmed or taken away again. Our relationship was safe, and God had already promised a rich friendship for our future. But now was not the time. When a king knights a royal servant, he is sending him out from the kingdom to accomplish a mission. Likewise, God was sending me out to be the mother of John Kelty, giving me the courage to leave the throne room and entrust Anna to her heavenly Father. I wish I had understood that message at the time. Though I had been knighted with courage, I fearfully kept my hand on the sphere, and I wasn't free to love our new John as fully as I could have.

## THE FEAR AND A PROMISE

September 15, 2005 – Journal entry

I am a nervous wreck. I haven't slept in two nights. I am so worried about baby John. As I plead for him to move, sometimes I call out Anna's name instead. I want her 36-week-old foot to jab me on the right side under my ribs, her signature move, so badly. My life feels so scary. I can't imagine or believe that good will come to us. It feels ridiculous to ask God for such a gift, knowing He allowed it to be taken from me before. But I will cry out to you, Jesus, in total fear and desperation. Do not remove your hand from my life or your breath from this baby. God, I'm begging you. Bring forth your restoration, goodness, faithfulness, and a measure of your redemption. As you did for Job, restore all that was lost. Please Lord, give me a word of encouragement, a truth, and a promise to cling to for peace when I am overcome with fear. Make this baby a healthy, big, and strong little guy. Make him a fighter. I know I am tangled up in believing so many lies about You, yet I am not even sure what they are…I feel so confused. Forgive me for so easily believing the enemy. Forgive me for trusting You so timidly. Keep fear far from me, Lord…. Sustain this baby's life!

I was afraid, and I was desperate. I asked God to give me a promise to cling to, and not long after I prayed this prayer, He provided me with an answer in a dream. My Granddaddy Sloop had been a very special man to me, in his life and in his death. I described earlier his white beard and his heart for God. I didn't mention, however, his signature flannel shirt and black beret. They were his daily uniform, even in the summer, and in my dream he wore them proudly:

> I was sitting in an unknown room at a table, and my Granddaddy walked through the door. I ran to him, and his hug and kiss were exactly as I'd remembered. "What are you doing here?" I asked. "Jesus has sent me to you. What do you want to ask of God?" Without hesitating I said, "I want world peace." I responded as if answering a question for the interview phase of a beauty pageant. I suppose it seemed like the appropriate, unselfish response. "No," he said. "God wants to know what *you* want." I was on God's personal agenda, and my Granddaddy was the messenger. Without hesitating and with a trembling heart, I replied, "I want this baby…I want this baby to live." Granddaddy smiled, satisfied

by my answer. He pulled out a piece of paper and a pen from his pocket, bent over the table, and began scribbling furiously. When he finished, he handed it to me. On one side these words were printed: *I came that they may have and enjoy life, and have it in abundance (John 10:10 AMP)*. On the other side was a drawing. There were several images that resembled gift bags, but at the same time they looked like suitcases; I couldn't decide which. Then I pleaded, "What does it mean?" He just smiled with a knowing look and a mischievous grin as he placed the beret on his shiny bald head. I looked up and said, "Please don't go." Without explanation or dramatic good-bye, he just walked out the door as if to say, "My work here is done."

"To have and enjoy life… in abundance": this was the promise I'd beseeched God for, for baby John. The fact that this verse was recorded in the gospel of *John* made the promise especially precious. I clung to it in every moment when fear overcame me during the remaining months of my pregnancy.

Before Granddaddy died, he was eager to greet his Savior and my Granny who had gone before him. He would declare in his cute little manner, "I'm getting ready for my trip without suitcases." John's original due date was the first anniversary of Anna's death, February 22, 2006. John was born four weeks early, arriving on January 23, 2006, the thirteenth anniversary of my Granddaddy's death. The little dream game of Pictionary between Granddaddy and me had been God's creative way of showing me He had a plan. The drawing of the gift bags and suitcases illustrated that John would be taking his first "big trip without suitcases" on the day Granddaddy took his last.

That was the gift. What a day to be born, and what a legacy to follow – January 23rd – a birthday into eternal life and a birthday into earthly life.

## FIRST DAYS WITH NEW LIFE

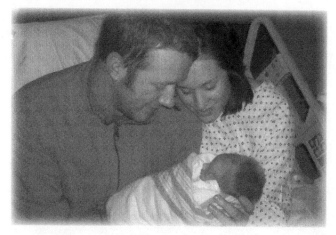

*Chris, Kate and baby John*

January 30, 2006 – Journal Entry

One week ago our son was born. He's alive! I barely know how to process all that has taken place. John is sweet and strong. He sleeps all the time, which I am told is normal for a preemie, yet he seems to have strength beyond his days. I love him so much, yet I am terribly frustrated that my love for him is in the same bag with crazy hormones and other very strong emotions including guilt, insecurity, and a fresh, stinging layer of grief.

When I think back on those first days of mothering baby John, I am overcome with disappointment. Nothing that I had wanted, other than John's safe delivery, was taking place in my soul. My emotions were in charge, navigating strange and unexpected behaviors in and around me. I felt foreign to myself and unable to lasso my heart. I was a hostage to my fears and the pain that endured. I was robbed of many of the precious experiences I had daydreamed about and had longed for. I was afraid of John-John. He weighed only five pounds, and his little legs looked like twigs I'd snapped in half as a child, making birthday candles for mud pies. I was embarrassed that I didn't know how to take care of him and got defensive when anyone tried to help me nurse, change his diaper, burp him, etc. I pushed everyone away, including my mother, to protect time with this baby. I was still so afraid he might take his last breath at any moment. How would I feel if he were in another's arms when he died? What I once would've seen as irrational was now a very real possibility. It had, after all, happened before.

I thought love would be enough and that fear would dissipate when a baby was safe in my arms. I soon learned that pregnancy fear was just the beginning, as fearing became a new normal, a constant, dark shadow following me everywhere.

The other predominant sadness I felt was the overwhelming grief that remained and the guilt that lingered for loving another baby. I felt like I was being unfaithful to Anna for any tenderness and love expressed to John. I felt a strong need to cling to Anna because I wanted to prove to myself and to the world that the vacuum she had left in my life couldn't be filled by a new baby. Every night after I laid John down in his crib, I would go and get my favorite picture of Anna, kiss her, and then sing her lullaby. I was terrified of moving on and what it would cost me. The road to eradicating these feelings would be a long one.

Every new and special encounter with John, from first baths and smiles to first birthday cakes and balloons, was a painful milestone I had never reached with Anna. I wished with all of my heart that I could separate the two because I knew that grief was robbing my joy with John, but I couldn't help it.

I was jealous of Chris, whose love affair with John wasn't complicated by his love for Anna. He had been able to separate his delight and suffering from his children in a way that I couldn't. I remember when I was pregnant with John hearing other mothers talk about the frustrations of crying babies and sleepless nights and blouses drenched in spit-up. I knew I would never be "one of those mothers." I reasoned that grieving mothers cherished their children and had room and grace for little annoyances that other mothers simply could not. Oh how wrong I was, and how quickly I became "one of those mothers." Hormones and exhaustion grabbed the wheel and took me on an awful ride.

From the beginning, John was an intense little boy. I remember sitting in the pediatrician's office and hearing a newborn baby cry in the next room. John's shrill squawks sounded nothing like the traditional newborn cries I'd heard before. It wasn't long until we learned that his shrieking indicated severe reflux that eventually led us to testing for cystic fibrosis. I was a nervous wreck. The results revealed that John simply struggled with significant reflux. His signature crying, bucking, and flailing indicated he was in pain. I felt frustrated that I couldn't help him and even more frustrated at my small reserve of tenderness and patience. After three different medications, we found one that helped tremendously, and at around ten months, the reflux was gone.

When John-John was six months old, Chris and I were faced with an enormous decision. Due to a variety of circumstances, a move back to my hometown in Virginia would be professionally and financially beneficial. We would be moving to Harrisonburg, a quaint college town where my mom and dad lived. I knew it would be difficult to move away from a place I'd called home for nearly ten years. We were also leaving Chris's family and the friends who had been our greatest support during the worst time of our life. It was such a bittersweet decision, but we knew where the ball was rolling, and we followed it to Virginia.

Saying good-bye to Kentucky forced me to say good-bye to Anna in new ways. Our house had allowed us to make a memorial room for her. To anyone else, it just looked like a lovely guest room. I bought a gold bedspread that matched one of the squares of fabric on the vintage quilt that had hung over her crib. Now the quilt lay across the end of the bed. I hung a shelf over the bed displaying six picture frames with the scriptures that had been in her room, the words of the song I'd written for her, and a couple of other special songs as well. Fifty dried pink and yellow roses sat in a vase along with several other treasures. Packing up her room was excruciating. I was saying good-bye to a haven of comfort and the symbolism that our family had space for her whether she was here or not. Life was forcing us to move on. My sister helped me and wrote Anna's name beautifully on several boxes, drawing tiny hearts next to her name. When the duct tape went on, I knew I wouldn't be opening them again for a very long time. As I write now, they are unopened in my grandparents' basement. One day I may have the privilege of bringing those boxes back to our house to decorate a nursery for another daughter, but as of now, they are collecting dust.

As we pulled away from the house, I tried to share a tender grief moment with Chris. He was distracted and preoccupied, and I knew in that moment that the tides had changed and that saying good-bye to Kentucky was turning the page to a new chapter in our lives. Chris was eager to get there. Our ships began to sail in different directions. Holding onto grief would keep me from Chris as he tried to move on with his life.

That was August 5, 2006. We unplugged ourselves from Lexington and tried to re-plug quickly into Harrisonburg. It was easier for Chris than for me. I nestled into our new house and tried to suck every ounce of joy out of decorating, painting, and repainting rooms. But I felt so alone, and my loose ends were unraveling. Not soon after our move, the leaves began to change, and cold settled in over the Shenandoah Valley. Winter was coming, and with it, an unruly and viscous storm of fear. This would prove to be the longest winter of my life.

CHAPTER 11

# THE LONGEST WINTER

*There is a time for everything and a season for*
*every activity under heaven. A time to be born*
*and a time to die. A time to weep and a time to*
*laugh. A time to mourn and a time to dance.*

*Ecclesiastes 3:1-2,4*

Fall 2006 – Journal Entry

Eighteen months after Anna

Dear God,

Something is hindering me. For over a year now, I have
sought You in crisis mode, pursuing a God I knew I
needed for healing, comfort, and peace. Rarely did I
pursue You for the sake of simply loving You, but to
figure You out. I felt justified in this loveless pursuit
because I was wounded. As I read now about a God
who loves so much, I feel reluctant and even unable
to pursue You in love. Crisis-mode was a "have to,"
whereas love mode is a "want to." God, do I want to? I
guess deep within me I am still so nervous about You.
Something makes me want to hide, just peeking out
from around the corner every now and again like a little
girl, intrigued but afraid.

My mind and some of my experiences tell me You are love, or maybe it's the Holy Spirit testifying the truth to my spirit. But my heart, the wounded part, the Anna part, hears a voice saying, "Careful now, He's dangerous and unruly and can't be trusted." Anna's death in no way seems loving or good and kind. God, you confuse me. How do I reconcile this tragedy into the equation of Your love I was once so sure of? Before Anna died, the resounding question of my soul was, "Am I worthy of God's love? Will God love me in spite of who I am?" Now the question seems to be, "Is God truly loving, and will I love Him in spite of who He is…sovereign?" What in the world does the sovereignty of God mean, anyway? Whatever it is, I know I am fighting against it.

My spiritual life feels like a game of cards. Until now I've had a fairly good hand. And then Anna died. Now that awful card of death is a permanent fixture in my hand that I cannot discard. This tragic event is a stain in the history of my life. How do I keep playing cards with this joker, a jester that appears to be one of the unpleasant faces of God? How do I continue to live, knowing there are other jokers cackling and waiting in the deck?

I guess it's a matter of choice. It has to be. This side of heaven, I will never understand Anna's death or accept it as God's calculated plan for my life. If I believe that, then it seems that I have to conclude that God is cruel. If the Bible declares that God is love, then I have no choice than to believe it, because I know that God's word is true and infallible. I know God is the answer, I just don't know Him. Will I ever trust God again?

Since John's birth, I had been coasting on the truths of my visions from before he was born. There were no new truths to draw upon or intimate moments with God to nourish me. Running on empty, my last and final arguments with God kept me from refueling. Soon I came to a screeching halt. All I could see were the prevailing images of the scary face of a God who seemed to have blown calamity into my life as effortlessly as a child blowing out candles on a birthday cake. I resonated with C.S. Lewis's words from <u>A Grief Observed</u>, "Not that I am (I think) in much danger of ceasing to believe in God. The real danger is of coming to believe such dreadful things about him. The conclusion I dread is not 'So there's no God after all,' but 'so this is what God's really like. Deceive yourself no longer.'"[7]

I tried to *feel* like I'd remembered and at times pursued God, pretending all was well. I had minimal success. Again and again, my darkest questions burst in like a thief, bagging my treasures of truth and leaving me scared and alone to face the enormity of my fears.

There had been so much healing, but still, words like "sovereignty" and "trust" were boulders dropped daily on the feet of my faith. I couldn't get past them, and now my life was occupied in such a way that I was unable to pursue God as I had in the beginning. Before, there had been no

---

[7] C.S. Lewis, *A Grief Observed* (United Kingdom: Faber and Faber) 1961, p 6-7.

agenda but to wake up and put one foot in front of the other. Now with a baby to tend to and a demanding life and schedule occupying my time, the pursuit of knowing God was put aside. Also, being in Virginia kept me from my friends who knew me, could read me, and would remind me to tend to my wounds. It was easy to keep things on the surface now that we only talked on the phone, and they couldn't see my face.

My marriage was different also. During the first year after our loss, Chris's main priority was taking care of his despondent wife and himself. His days were erased of everything that required responsibility other than "us." Now with a son to adore and a vocation to pursue, grief didn't easily fit into his life. He needed a companion full of joy and trust, one who would hold his hand and pull him along toward a future bursting with promise. He simply needed a healed wife and the helpmate he had married. But I was far from ready to let go of the crutch he had become for me. Chris was ready to relinquish that role which weighed him down and kept him burdened under a heavy coat of depression. For me, the coat represented pain, but also comfort and intimacy with Chris that I was far from ready to shed. The comfort that came from being separate from the world but in it together felt like a thing of the past. I grieved for our marriage. Pain was, strangely, the sweetest glue we had known. His change was inevitable though; we couldn't live that way forever. Chris was simply ready to take that step before I was. I watched from the dock as his ship sailed in search of better waters. For the first time in our shared loss, I felt utterly alone. How would I function without my doting companion?

Chris didn't attribute his love for Anna to the presence of his pain. He had not bought into that lie. He was ready to shed daily mourning. He also didn't seem to be spiritually tormented like I was. Later I would come to realize that the love Chris had once given me so abundantly in grief had kept me from longing for a greater and more complete love from God.

The New Year came, winter pushed on, and 2007 was underway. John turned one at the end of January, Anna would have been two at the end of February, and baby number three was conceived at the beginning of March. There was new excitement, but the dam holding back the floodgates of fear was about to break. Pregnancy was a treacherous mountain with few props to secure the trail. What would the third journey bring?

It had been two years. My confusion and anger toward God had created distance between me and that first year's visions and encounters with Christ. I decided the feelings I had could never go away, so I learned to function around them. But functioning became harder as my belly grew bigger, and baby Ben slept for nine months, with barely a kick in my womb. With each inhaled breath came the worry of wondering if he were dead or alive. I approached God out of total fear. He held the power to curse or bless my life, and I was terrified to cross Him. I felt certain that the only way to manage life was to take all matters into my own hands. I couldn't trust God to protect my children, but neither could I protect nor provide for a baby I couldn't yet hold. My increasing panic led to yet another early delivery, and Benjamin Kyle was safe in my arms on November 9, 2007.

*Kate and Baby Ben*

The peace I felt and the breath I took the moment he was born brought me quite possibly the greatest sense of relief I have ever known. I will never forget the night Ben was born. The nurse brought him to me to feed. In my foggy state, I had forgotten that he had arrived, and I held him and nursed him for an hour. The smile never left my face. Now I was a seasoned mother. The insecurity was gone. The uncomplicated joy I'd longed for when John was born overcame me, and I simply reveled in every second of it. Finally, with the third birth, there was an exuberance of joy and peace.

The next few weeks at home were precious with our boys. I was tired, but I was so enamored with my little guys. Their personality differences were already evident. I daydreamed about the future. I could so easily imagine a house full of sweaty neighborhood boys, a table spread with their favorite snacks and drinks, John and Ben lingering for a kiss and a thank-you as their friends headed to the backyard with a football under their arms. Life, for a small season, felt good.

Unfortunately, winter resumed, and Anna's third birthday loomed in the distance. The clarity and simplicity didn't last as the complicated fog of grief crept in and clouded my dreams. I didn't have time to be happy; there was too much to be afraid of. This time the fear came back with a vengeance, and I was terrified of absolutely everything. Driving the car was a waking nightmare. I pictured wrecks and the injuries of my children at every intersection. The grocery store was even worse. I was convinced that every man behind me in line had followed me there and was plotting his abduction of me and my boys. I planned my attack and my rescue efforts before I even realized what I was doing. But I was most controlled by the fear of sudden, inexplicable death. I checked on Ben ten times a night. I couldn't rest until I had checked on him again and again. I envisioned disaster and loss. I was exhausted from my efforts to protect my children from events over which I had no control. I was tormented.

From the beginning, Ben was a sweet and contented baby. However, Ben was not a good sleeper. I have never been more tired in my life. To make matters worse, I became ill with mononucleosis the week of Anna's third birthday and endured ten days of severe sore throat and sickness. I refused to take any pain medication due to nursing. There were two months of complete exhaustion after that. I was a miserable mess. I felt anxious and agitated all the time. I was snapping at John, and I felt embarrassed and angry at my inability to be patient and wise with him.

As Anna's third birthday approached, my body went back in time and relived the days and moments leading up to her death. The panic was awful, and the sense that I needed to do something to stop it was great. I felt like I was standing on the beach all alone trying to push back the winds and waves of an approaching tsunami. I felt responsible and unable to distance myself from the panic. I couldn't think rationally. As soon as February 22, 2008 came, death day, I woke up and I said, "It is finished." I continued to live sadly, but without the terror of impending doom. Anna had died for the third year in a row, and there was nothing I could do to deny or reverse that reality.

I looked at my children and found a measure of joy in their existence, yet I knew something was missing. I was numb and on the edge of *losing it* all the time. I kept a good deal of the agony to myself because I didn't want to frighten anyone, especially Chris. But I was scared of who I was becoming.

## JESUS

The week after Ben was born, I started a new small group Bible study. At the time, I had no idea how desperately I was in need of the fellowship and camaraderie. I took what felt like a risk and opened up to the group about the pain I was in and the terror that was overtaking my life as Anna's birthday drew near.

As I shared my lament and a recent vision over the loss of Anna, the conversation led to revelation. I had not yet understood the vision and was nervous to dissect it. My new friends gave me the courage to present it to them, and they shared their tears and thoughts as to what the Lord might be speaking to me. It was insight that would take me to the threshold of the healing I had been resisting for three years.

It had been a long time since I had seen Jesus. Not because He wasn't there, but because I had stopped seeking His face. Fear and worry tempted to devour my faith and the beautiful, true image of Jesus I had worked so hard to establish. A thick fog had settled in. I could barely see my hands, much less the Savior who stood before me. I hadn't rehearsed truth in so long, and the presence of fear and the accompanying lies was like a can of black paint that had spilled over the top of my canvas of Christ. My friends and our new study pushed me to His word and encouraged a prayer that ushered me into His presence. We were simply to say over and over, "Make your home in me." As I repeated the phrase, the blank, dark page before me was infiltrated with light, and I knew I was moments away from seeing Jesus.

I was standing in an unknown house looking into what appeared to be the study of the home. There was a large mahogany desk in the center of the room, and the walls stretched up high, each with bookshelves that reached the ceiling. I stood with curiosity peering into the room. Jesus stepped out from behind the desk. I knew at that moment that this room was Christ's home in my heart. He was in what appeared to be the home office of my soul, and He was waiting for me. "Give it to me." At His request I looked down to find a black vase in my hands. It was a tall vase that narrowed at the top. Dark but majestic, it looked as though it had been hand-made and carefully detailed with dark shades of night. Jesus then pointed to the top of one of the shelves, and I saw several vases just like it, but in shades of pale blue swirled with white, as if the artist had dipped his paint brush into the sky. They were truly works of art, beautiful and tranquil. I knew He wanted to make a trade, mine for His. But for some reason, I was reluctant to let go. Finally I handed Him the vase, and He handed me one of His. He motioned for me to breathe into the opening of the vase. As I bent my head to the mouth of the vase, a vapor escaped and filled my nose. It felt like a breath I'd dreamed of but had never taken before. I felt instantly alive and satiated with peace. Pleased, Jesus took my black vase and hurled it onto the floor, and it shattered into a hundred tiny pieces. As it broke, I felt a rip in my heart, and I gasped with an aching and urgent sense that something was terribly wrong. Whatever Jesus had broken, I desperately wanted to fix. I wanted to drop to my knees, pick up every fragment of pottery, and put it back together. It seemed like my life depended on it. But then again, I knew that if Jesus had broken it, it could only have been right.

I opened my eyes and began sobbing. Something was realized in my heart, something I didn't yet understand but knew was the next puzzle God had for me to piece together.

It became apparent that the black vase represented my fear, a weapon of protection in a relationship with a God I didn't trust. I was toting it around like a pistol in the hands of a traumatized war veteran, tormented by visions of a haunted past. The only way to protect my family from danger was to fear and to be on guard against every possible, tragic scenario. It was a scary way to live, but trust was the only other option. I felt certain that trusting God would only lead to greater disappointment and would leave me exposed and vulnerable to unknown enemies. The black vase had become my security blanket, giving me a false sense of safety in an unsafe world. For Jesus to break it was to take away my safety and security. I had yet to realize that the one who had guaranteed peace and protection with his black vase was the enemy. The father of all lies, opposed to freedom, and the one who *comes to steal, kill and destroy (John 10:9)* had a hook in me. I had bought into the seduction of the craftiest killer of all.

The blue vase, promising peace, was there all along but had gotten too high up on the shelf of my soul for me to be able to reach it alone. I inhaled the faint sweetness of its aroma, peace and freedom, but was so attached to my dark vase that letting go was inconceivable. In time, I learned the deeper meaning behind the pottery. The vases, though constructed similarly, were much more than fear and peace. They represented trust, trust in God versus trust in self. I couldn't hold them both at once. The vision showed me that my new normal was dangerous and was a counterfeit for the true protection and security I was seeking. I needed help to get free from the web that entangled me. Now I knew I was stuck. Becoming un-stuck seemed the necessary task. I didn't trust Jesus. I had made that clear from the very beginning and had never reestablished myself as a trusting, dependent child of God.

In the beginning, Jesus manifested Himself to me in such powerful ways. The truth that these experiences with Him deposited in my spirit had been locked with a key of fear and anger. Accessing the power of these truths was nearly impossible.

The vision enlightened me about how broken I truly was and how spiritually paralyzed I had become. I wanted to get well and become whole, and I knew I needed help. I wasn't sure whom to turn to, but I received the name of a man who had lost his wife to cancer and specialized in grief counseling.

After a two-year sabbatical from the pursuit of resurrecting my view of God and the longest winter I had ever known, I was once again back on course. As I approached the front lines for battle, I was unable to see that Jesus was waiting with giddy delight as His little girl, hands on her hips, scowl on her face, marched her way home.

# PART FOUR

# SAVIOR

# CHAPTER 12

# YOU ARE SAFE

*For we are not wrestling with flesh and blood but against
the world rulers of this present darkness...against the
spirit forces of wickedness in the heavenly sphere....*

*Ephesians 6:12-13 (AMP)*

*No one ever told me that grief felt so like fear.*[8]

*C.S. Lewis ~ A Grief Observed*

I instantly liked my new counselor Jim. He was kind, gentle, and wise. The fact that he had endured the very painful loss of his beloved wife made me feel known and understood by him instantly. Any worry I had about being able to adequately explain my grief vanished. I explained my loss of Anna and how the years had unraveled since. I described the frightening realm I was living in and the persistent, unwanted battle I was waging with God. I had seen and tasted His goodness, yet I still fought. Why did He allow it? What would He continue to allow? How could I trust God when He seemed to wear His sovereignty like a superhero's cape? I lamented, I vented, and I wept.

He asked if he could pray for me, and when I closed my eyes, as if no time had passed, I was once again on the visual path to healing I had traveled so intimately before:

---

[8]   C.S. Lewis, A Grief Observed (United Kingdom: Faber and Faber) 1961, p 6-7.

To my left, I saw the dark silhouette of a person pulling back on reins of some kind. My eyes traced them to the right to discover an object held in place with the reins wrapped around it. It appeared to be a slingshot. Then I saw that the ropes continued to the right past the object, and Jesus stood holding the reins on the other side. It wasn't a sling shot. It was a game of tug-of-war, and my heart was bound in the middle.

As we continued to pray, I saw a second image. I was standing naked, encircled by a camp of savages pointing arrows at me. There was nowhere to turn, nowhere to escape.

Instantly I knew that the ropes represented the fear strangling my heart: fear that made me feel exposed, surrounded by a team of advancing, angry warriors. I was viewing life and viewing God as an enemy preparing to take me out. Fear, the only possible reaction, provided a weapon against such danger.

Going back to the first image, the counselor said he felt specifically led to ask God a question about the vision. He asked if that would be okay. I nodded, and I heard him speak these words, "Lord, is it important for us to know the name of the figure to the left?" As soon as I heard his prayer, I knew he thought the dark figure represented Satan. That hadn't even occurred to me as I had already surmised that the mystery figure tugging war against Jesus for my heart was, in fact, me. *Wasn't it my battle with him?* Though I felt certain of my conclusion, I still closed my eyes and waited for clarity to emerge.

With the eyes of my heart, I turned to my right where I knew Jesus stood and asked, "Lord, does the figure have a name?" I stared at Jesus, expecting to see His mouth move to form the sound of my name, when from behind me and in my left ear I heard, "It is I, Lucifer!"

Panting, I opened my eyes to escape the vision, like a scared child darting out of a dark room, convinced she had seen a monster. Except this wasn't my imagination. Satan, by the power and authority of Jesus, had come out of hiding and answered my question. I sat trembling and tearful, trying to catch my breath, gathering the courage to speak what had just taken place.

As I shared the terrifying interchange that had just occurred in the spirit world, the counselor didn't look at all surprised. I think he was relieved that my eyes and ears had been opened to what he suspected, so that something could be done to regain my freedom. He prayed simply, "Stand back, Lucifer, by the authority of Jesus."

At that, I saw Jesus stretch back the reins of the war ropes and let go. The bands whirled with a vengeance toward my captor and pierced the chest of the enemy, who flew back at the impact and then dissipated. I looked up to see my heart plummeting to the ground, having been tossed into the air from the release of the enemy's reins. Jesus rushed to catch my heart just before it hit the dirt. Pulling my soul into the safety of His chest, He looked at me and tenderly proclaimed with authority, *you are safe.*

As I opened my eyes to my physical reality, I sat in total shock and bewilderment with a sense of freedom that I find hard to explain. I remember the counselor sharing with me later that fear is an enormous part of grief and that strongholds are often formed in the caverns left by death and loss. I had been in a spiritual battle, and I hadn't even realized that Satan had been camping out in my pain and feeding me lies about God, encasing me in wretched fear. I had just assumed that what I had been experiencing was the natural and expected outcome of such a loss. Now my enlightened mind recalled the verse, *Be self-controlled and alert, your enemy the devil prowls around like a roaring lion looking for someone to devour (1 Peter 5:8).* I was weak, grieving, and untrusting of God—I was easy prey.

That evening when I returned home, everything looked and felt different. It was as if the sun had suddenly risen on my life, chasing the darkness into the night where it belonged. How long had it been since I had seen the light of day? How long had I navigated life, hunted by ghosts and their shrieking lies? How long had I feared God and sought to be my own protector? As I climbed into bed that evening, I looked at Chris, and I felt all sorts of joy knowing a new road was ahead for us both. I lay my head down on my pillow, ready to enter sleep free from nightmares. I suddenly remembered that I had not checked on the children, and I sat up quickly to complete my evening ritual, motivated by fear. But I stopped when I realized the fear was gone. All that was left was a bad habit to break. I lay my head back down on the pillow, snuggling into the new peace and security that had been granted to me, a holy blanket of peace. Yes, it was true; I was finally safe.

I had been a hostage to fear, not realizing there was a way out. I assumed fear was an unwelcome but permanent entity in my life, the result of grief. But now I realized that a war for my heart had raged since childhood. I saw it all so clearly, that *my struggle was not against flesh and blood, but against spiritual forces of wickedness (Ephesians 6:12-13),* but now I knew how to fight and that my avenger was greater and more powerful than my enemy.

## THE TRUE GOD

A week later I returned to counseling without any trepidation. I was excited to take the next steps forward on my healing journey and to enter into greater freedom. I was also eager to process something new I had learned. My counselor had given me an assignment at the end of our session the week before which opened my eyes to an astounding realization about the way I viewed and therefore related to God. He had given me a chart with forty different positive characteristics of God. I was to check the degree to which each attribute aligned with my personal view of Him. I began the questionnaire and quickly found myself stuck. I couldn't settle on an answer because, for me, God and Jesus were two very different people. Each time I would make a decision about who Jesus was, I would think of how I viewed God and would change my mind.

Jesus, to me, represented kindness, gentleness, and compassion, but was weak and powerless. God, on the other hand, was strong, but also controlling and angry at His own creation. He allowed His own son to suffer an excruciating death on a cross, even as Jesus cried out to Him, "My God, My God, why have you forsaken me?" (Matthew 27:45-46).

I was stunned as the reality of my feelings about God appeared on the assignment in front of me. Jesus had been a lifeline to me in my grief, but God had not. I was open to and grateful for the love of Jesus, but all I felt about God was a great desire to distance myself from his tyrannical rule. Upon this realization, I read and reread the scripture, "The Father and I are one. If you have seen Me you have seen the Father." (John 10:30). But I couldn't sort it out. I couldn't feel about God the way I felt about Jesus. My counselor began to gently correct my view of God. Knowing that my perception of Him would block my great need for healing, he helped me to realize that the God I perceived was a creation of my own mind. He then led me into a new understanding of God the Father.

In his book Ruthless Trust, Brennan Manning writes it more perfectly than I could ever attempt: "Jesus alone reveals who God is. We cannot deduce anything about Jesus from what we think we know about God. However, we must deduce everything we know about God from what we know about Jesus. This implies that all of our prevailing images and understandings of God must crumble in the earthquake of Jesus' self-disclosure."[9]

As the peace, freedom, wisdom, and love began to multiply, I knew I was on the right path. I was finally pursuing and being won over by the God I had always longed to know, *Jesus, the visible image of the invisible God (Colossians 3:1).*

As I pondered this revelation, that Jesus was in fact God, I realized that the loss of Anna hadn't created my distorted view of Him, but rather exposed and exacerbated the false image that was already there. Satan's greatest weapon against me was taunting me with the lies he had already planted in my heart.

---

[9] Manning, Brennan. Ruthless Trust: The Ragamuffins Path to God (SanFrancisco, HarperSanFrancisco; A Division of HarperCollins Publishers) 2000, p.88.

He knew that my pain and grief would fertilize his once hidden deceits until a completely false view of God the Father grew.

Now I stared without reluctance into the true face of God, who is Jesus. However, I still needed to uproot a few lies that had embedded themselves within me. I believed Jesus to be weak because He hadn't stepped in to prevent my loss of Anna. I had bought into a philosophy that Anna's death was an accident, as if it had happened when God's back was turned. I wanted to believe this because to entertain any other reason for Anna's death would mean I would have to come face to face with God's sovereignty and grapple with the idea that He had *allowed and agreed* for it to happen.

The counselor encouraged me to begin a conversation with Jesus about what it would mean if *He* were sovereign, turning my ear from the previous uncaring god I'd been perceiving. As I left counseling that day, the new assignment was to begin to *seek Jesus and Jesus alone*, to abandon the God I had been relating to and hiding from, the God who was clearly not the Jesus of *the Way, the Truth and the Life (John 14:6)*.

For the first time in my grief journey, I began to intentionally address Jesus with every prayer and question, especially questions about His control in and over my life. Somehow I sensed that coming to understand His sovereign goodness would be the final and missing component to making peace with God.

I had spent the first year after my loss carefully uncovering the truth of my Savior with my visions as a guide. With this new revelation, I was finally able to access the mantle of my heart and replace the distorted image of "God" with my new work in progress, *the face of Jesus*. With a long, painful, and disillusioned break, I was ready to pick up the brush and finish that which I had so painfully and supernaturally begun.

## THE SPARK

God was clearly leading me into a renewal of my relationship with Him. It wasn't just about grief or Anna anymore. It was really all about Jesus and me. A coffee date with a friend in grief would bring yet another eye-opening and heart-mending realization to light.

Tracy had been widowed after seven years of marriage. She had two small children. The cup from which she had drunk seemed utterly unbearable. It had been seven years since her tragedy; I arranged a coffee date to glean truth from this woman who seemed so radiant and unburdened. She exuded peace, and I was intrigued that she didn't wear her suffering like I did. I felt she must have some secret truth she could share, and I was grateful for the opportunity to sip wisdom from the cup of her life.

Two hours passed with barely a blink as I peered into her eyes and took notes with my heart. As I walked away, I knew exactly how Tracy was different from me. She had accepted her life with all of its wounds and scars and had fallen in love with Jesus in riveting ways as a result of her loss. She knew Him as her rescuer and her redeemer, and she had embraced her true purpose for living, to exalt and exemplify the One she loved. As she talked about Jesus there was a light in her eyes, an effervescent joy that sparked a longing deep within me to be fully satisfied by God and to be free from the poison of unresolved suffering. As she smiled, cried, and laughed, I was ready to be done, to remove from my life whatever I needed to claim the beauty and redemption Tracy had found. I ached for it. Whatever she had, I knew I was born for, and the fragrance of it made me long for more.

My release from fear and from the false god I'd created, as well as my inspiring conversation with Tracy, worked like yeast in the warm dough of my heart. I sensed I was being prepared for a new season, one I'd been searching and longing for all my life.

# CHAPTER 13

# SPRING AT LAST

*After the suffering of His soul He will see*
*the light of life and be satisfied.*

*Isaiah 53:11*

*My ears had heard of You, but now my eyes have seen You.*

*Job 4:2-4*

I couldn't have been more than five years old when we got lost in the woods behind our small Georgia home. Of course, I had no idea I was lost. Granddaddy had come to visit and decided he would take his three grandchildren for a walk. Our home backed up to the thick woods, and we often adventured there, following the familiar paths, making up stories as we would go. This particular day was beautiful. The woods opened up into a vast green meadow with one sprawling, majestic tree in the center. I think this was the first moment in my life when I felt captivated by something beautiful. I can see it so clearly, the bright sky and the exquisite tree, and walking up to it with my little fingers tightly woven into the strong, warm hand of my granddaddy. I remember looking up at him in awe, the warmth that emanated from his smile matching the sun. This day was pure delight. When we reached a stranger's home and sat in the kitchen while granddaddy made a phone call, it still didn't occur to me that we were lost. I just thought we were meeting someone new, which would not have been out of character for my granddaddy. It wasn't until I saw my dad pulling into the stranger's driveway with a panic-stricken face that I realized something was wrong. I never knew I was lost, because I was perfectly at home in the care of the one I was with.

*Katie and Granddaddy Sloop*

For years, I had been lost. When Anna died, it was as if I had been hurled from the sky, down into the ferocious wilderness of grief. At first I had questioned whether God was with me. Hadn't He thrust me into this darkness? Hadn't he abandoned me? But one truth at a time, I came to discover the true heart of the One I was with. After several years of grieving and fighting with Him, I came to know Him, and in knowing Him I realized I wasn't lost at all. After years of wandering, I could joyfully proclaim I was home.

August 22, 2008 – Journal Entry

I am full of something…it feels like hope, as if I'm alive for the first time in a long time. Like a bulb lying dormant under the cold earth, suddenly pushing a tulip into the spring sunlight. Something woke up. I feel alive. I feel energized to know God and to discover Him. He is no longer to blame. My soul has acquitted Him. I'm not exactly sure how it happened, but He is my champion. I wrongly accused Him for so long, but no matter, He is my champion still. The pieces have come together, and I realize I do love Him, and His good hand has been here all along.

There was peace with God, and with that peace came courage. For months, at my counselor's suggestion, I had been asking Jesus to reveal to me what His sovereignty meant. It was an enormous theological mountain to climb, yet I knew understanding God's sovereignty in and over the circumstances of my life was imperative to my healing. My dad very simply explained that sovereignty means nothing takes God by surprise, that all things are under His *loving* control. His omniscience (that He is all-knowing), His omnipresence (that He is ever present), and His omnipotence (that He is all-powerful) are the components of His sovereignty. I was ready for Jesus to show me what it all meant, the holy "allow" that had shattered my life.

God began to show me that His permission of tragedy didn't cancel out His goodness. I began to see the imprint of His hand in my life both before and after our loss. He revealed little evidences, sacred gifts, that He had always been in control and that He had a calculated plan for my pain and healing.

God opened my eyes to see that even when life felt unhinged, He had in fact *hemmed me in, behind and before (Psalm 139:5)*. I began to see His hands in my story, like parentheses, holding together the pieces of my past, present, and future. I no longer felt deconstructed, but rather perfectly held together. These revealed evidences of God's presence and plan for me are sacred reminders of how He can be so good in the midst of all that is so very wrong.

## I WILL BE WITH YOU

About a month before we lost Anna, I rocked in her nursery, my favorite nook in the house, having just finished a book on breastfeeding. I was suddenly overcome by a feeling I can only describe as doom. I prayed instantly, and my mind was opened to a memory from childhood:

> My mother and I were standing together beside a wooden sign that read "Highland Retreat." She was dropping me off for a week of summer camp, and I was crying because I didn't want to be away from her. I was seven. We had just moved to Virginia from Georgia, and I imagine I was feeling insecure. My mother pulled an object from her pocket and placed it in my hand, folding my fingers tightly around it. Curious, I opened my hand to find a dull copper penny. Then my mother said to me, "Katie, carry this penny in your pocket and feel for it each time you feel homesick. It will be a reminder of me and my love for you." Confused, I responded, "But what does a penny have to do with you?" Pointing to the engraving of the year the penny was made she said, "1979, that was the year you were born and became my

little girl. Nothing can ever change that fact even if we're apart." As she began to drive away, she rolled down the window and spoke words I had heard hundreds of times before, "Remember Katie-Kate, no matter what happens, your mama will always love you." I distinctly remember clutching the penny underneath my pillow that night, falling asleep within the safety of belonging and knowing I was loved.

Confused as to how this memory had anything to do with the sensation of doom I was feeling, I asked Jesus, "Lord, what was that all about?" The moment the prayer left my lips and my eyes closed, I saw Jesus:

He was standing across the room from me with one hand on Anna's crib, and He said, "I will be with you." Instantly the doom vanished, and the joy of anticipation returned.

I surmised that Jesus wanted me to know that just as my mother's love had been with me even though I couldn't see her, so Jesus was with me and would help me through the new journey of motherhood before me.

Within weeks of experiencing this warm and reassuring moment with Jesus, Anna was gone. Had Jesus lied to me? For years this vision had fueled my anger at God. Wasn't He promising to guide me and be with me as I entered motherhood? Now I saw the vision for what it really was: a loving, all-knowing Father, promising His presence when the doom I felt would one day soon become a reality. Just as my mother had sought to reassure me of her love when I was apart from her, Jesus sought to reassure me that in the moments when I would feel abandoned by Him, He was and would be, in fact, with me and for me. Now there was no guessing about it. God allowed Anna's death. He knew it would happen, but somehow it no longer made Him my enemy. It made Him the hero of every dark day in between.

In the beginning, I didn't know Jesus. I knew and feared the false god I had created, so it was easy to point the finger of blame. Now, I did know Him, Jesus, the true face of God, and this truth allowed me to embrace His knowing in a way that soothed my scars with peace. He knew. He had gifted me with a promise weeks before her death that He would be with me… and He was.

## Whispers From Jesus

I had been unable to muster the courage before, but now I was ready to read for the first time the journal that I had kept during the months I carried Anna. The journal was the written record of her life and our relationship. I had been apprehensive about revisiting these pages because I knew it would sweep me back into forgotten memories, the loss of innocent happiness, and the pain of her absence. But compelled by new healing and my friendship with Jesus, I opened our book and spent several hours with a pot of coffee and a box of tissues, reliving the prayer life of an expectant mother. What I found within the pages was the shocking and precious revelation that God had answered specific prayers I had prayed for Anna. Or rather, God had given me words with which to beseech Him, already knowing her eternal destiny.

July 9, 2004

I can't believe it. I'm pregnant. I'm in total shock. Even though I've been planning and praying, I'm still shocked. Protect our baby. I pray even now that the womb would be a testimony of your love.

September 16, 2004

Worship is a word that keeps coming to me…child of worship… that somehow even in the womb, this baby would understand how magnificent and holy You are and want to praise You. I know on a cognitive level he/she can't understand, but I pray as I worship and praise You myself, the baby would leap and rejoice. I also pray you would make the nursery a haven, a sanctuary where Your Spirit and Your angels would be pleased to come. I pray our baby would see angels and would be drawn into Your holiness. Thank you, Jesus!

October 19, 2004

I can hardly believe this is happening! I am so eager to know if we are having a daughter or a son. I pray that you would give me a special scripture for our baby, and I pray You would bring it to me in a divine way…a dream, a revelation. You know the glorious plans You have for this child. I cannot wait to watch it all unfold according to Your plan. And God, would You please give me the words to write a lullaby for our baby.

December 4, 2004

Dear Father,

Where do I even begin with all I have to say? I cannot believe in three-and-a-half months I will be holding the tiny baby girl You have placed in our care to love, to nurture, and to hold…to teach her eyes to see You, her hands to reach for You and to serve You, her feet to draw near to You and to draw unto all the places You have set for her to go. But most of all, for her heart to love You. What an enormous job. I ask myself, am I ready? I comfort myself with the truth that You long for me to be a mother even more than I long to be a mother.

As I sat with my pen and scribbled down earnest, loving prayers for my developing baby, God sat with me, too. I believe that God, who knows all things, who has infinite wisdom and immeasurable love, planted prayers for Anna in my heart. He knew the only opportunity I would have this side of heaven to mother Anna would be inside my womb, and He made it rich. I prayed that the nursery would be a place where angels would be pleased to come, and they did. I prayed Anna would be drawn into God's holiness, and she was. I prayed for dreams and revelations of the glorious plans God had for our baby girl, and He gave. I prayed for her eyes to see Him, her hands to reach for Him, her feet to draw near to Him, and her heart to love Him, and she does. And I prayed that God would use the womb as a testimony of His love, and He most certainly has, for me.

I am not saying I believe God orchestrated Anna's death as an answer to my prayers. I am saying, however, that He tenderly and sweetly gave me prayers for Anna as gifts of His all-knowing goodness. This aspect of God's sovereignty somehow gave me the strength of knowing I could survive. It wasn't an accident. He allowed, and there is no doubt in my mind that Jesus was the first to weep over our pain. I now believed with all of my heart that *God was working all things, (even the awful), together for my good (Romans 8:28).*

I clutched the journal against my chest and wept deep sobs of joy. Resurrection power was lifting me higher and higher as I embraced God's love more fully than I ever had.

## SUPERNATURAL TIMING

I was living in the springtime of love. My new revelations of God and receiving the sovereign gifts of His presence and love during my pregnancy made me feel like I had wings, especially after years of being bound by grief and unmerited hatred. I was invigorated to know God and to see as much as He would allow of His hand and presence through all the chapters of my grief.

One Sunday morning, I sat eagerly in the pew and opened my Bible at the pastor's invitation. He had a message to share from Revelation, chapter 12:

*Then I witnessed in heaven an event of great significance. I saw a woman clothed with the sun...She was pregnant, and she cried out because of her labor pains and the agony of giving birth. Then I saw a large red dragon with seven heads and ten horns...He stood in front of the woman as she was about to give birth, ready to devour her baby as soon as it was born. She gave birth to a son who was to rule all nations with an iron scepter. And her child was snatched away from the dragon and was caught up to God and to his throne. And the woman fled into the wilderness, where God had prepared a place to care for her for 1,260 days (Revelation 12:1-6).*

My heart began beating rapidly as I listened to words I had never read before, yet a vision had displayed its components to me, just weeks after our loss. In the third chapter, "The Anna Truths," I share my vision of the golden scepter, of watching Anna snatched up to God and His throne, of standing before Jesus and receiving His golden scepter. I was oblivious to anything else the pastor said that morning. I read over the passage again and again, one verse seizing my heart more than all the others: *And the woman fled into the wilderness, where God had prepared a place to care for her for 1,260 days (Revelation 12:6).*

For the rest of the afternoon I meditated on this scripture, returning to it again and again. Suddenly I was seized with knowing, and I grabbed my calculator and started to do the math. 1,260 is three and a half years. I grabbed my calendar and started counting. It was exactly three and a half years to the day from the moment Anna died, February 22, 2005, to the day in which I walked out into the full sunlight of God's healing love, recorded in my journal on August 22, 2008.

Just as the scripture proclaims that God had prepared a desert place to care for the woman who had lost her baby, snatched up to God in Revelation 12, so He had prepared a place for me for the same number of days. God knew the timing of it all. He knew the door of grief I would enter, and He knew the very moment, three and a half years into the distance, when I would exit in freedom. The vision of the golden scepter carried much more meaning, significance, and truth than I could possibly have comprehended at the time it was initially given. From truths about Anna, to truths about our preserved relationship, to the final healing layers of God's ultimate knowledge, the vision was a gift from the sovereign hand of God. Not only did He know death would happen, but He also knew the expanse of my wilderness and the exact moment I would exit in freedom.

I sat with my Bible and calendar on my lap and wept. My God had always had a plan. My God had always been in control. I didn't have to be. I finally understood, embraced, and loved the sovereign goodness of God, manifestations of His love. Before my loss had ever occurred, He had promised to be with me. During precious moments of my pregnancy, He gave me prayers He intended to fulfill. During the worst days of my grief, He gave me a vision and a scripture which revealed His calculated plan to set me free. I felt as though I were standing in the room among the twelve disciples as Jesus lovingly and boldly offered one of His final declarations: *I have told you these things so that in Me you may have peace. In this world you will have trouble, but take heart, I have overcome the world (John 16:33).* My life had seen a great deal of trouble, but Jesus had overcome my pain with the power of His love, and He was in control…and this meant I could not only survive, but thrive in my fallen world.

It seemed as though I were walking in my childhood meadow once again, holding the nail-scarred hand of Jesus, unaware of anything but His light and love. The words of a beloved psalm danced on the wind and encompassed my heart and mind: *Yea though I walk through the valley of the shadow of death, I will fear no evil, for You are with me (Psalm 23:4).* And finally, that was all that I needed.

# CHAPTER 14

# VICTORY DAY

*He will swallow up death in victory. He will abolish death
forever. And the Lord God will wipe away tears from all faces
and the reproach of His people. It shall be said in that day,
"Behold our God upon whom we have waited and hoped, that
He might save us! This is the Lord, we have waited for him...*

*Isaiah 25:8-9 (AMP)*

I couldn't believe how much peace had invaded my life by
my coming to understand and even love the sovereign qualities
of God. I couldn't get over it. I was overwhelmed with wonder
and joy at the ways He had been present and had intervened in
my life. But there was still one more truth, one more component
of God's sovereign goodness to be anchored in my heart – His
power and His ultimate victory.

I sat on the couch and bowed my head when the counselor
began our session in prayer. A moment later, I opened my eyes,
blinked, and sat quietly as I contemplated what I had just seen. I
was caught off guard when a horse and an apple appeared in my
mind. Reluctantly, I shared the seemingly insignificant images.

We continued to pray...

> I saw Jesus mounted on a vibrant horse on a carousel.
> He was inviting me to ride with Him. "Come on,
> Katie," He said with an extended hand and a smile.
> Signature braids revealed that I was about seven years
> old. Scanning the surroundings, I could tell we were at a

carnival, a place which has always been a bit unnerving to me. The sky was dark, and the atmosphere held an air of caution. A storm seemed to be brewing. Reluctantly, I took His hand, and He helped me up onto the horse in front of His. I observed that, unlike on a traditional merry-go-round, all the horses were positioned to face His. Within seconds, the suspended horse I was riding slid with lightning speed down the pole, crashing onto the rotating floor beneath it. I glared at Jesus, a piercing look of accusation. I thought to myself, "Why did He let the horse fall, and why didn't He put me on a different horse if He knew this would happen?" Knowing the blame and distrust materializing in my mind, Jesus, calm and unaffected, said, "But Katie, don't you see? The horse is still on the pole." Helping me onto another horse, Jesus and I continued to ride the carousel, this time successfully together. Lying on the ground in the dust beside the carousel was an apple missing one bite.

I knew immediately that the vision spoke to Christ's faithful presence with us during the "falls" of life. I also knew He intended to speak to me about His sovereignty once more when He spoke about the horse not falling off the pole. Though the horse had crashed, it had not fallen away from the pole, which represented God's ultimate control. But I had no idea about the apple, either why it lay next to the carousel or how it had gotten there.

A few days later I picked up a children's Bible given to my son Ben for his baptism. As I opened the book to the marked page, a naked and whimsical Eve appeared holding an apple missing one bite, with a conniving and crafty serpent slithering beneath her. The image of the apple burned in my mind as I remembered my vision and the similar apple that had mysteriously appeared beside the carousel. The next day I was finishing my Bible study, <u>Living Free,</u> and I came to these words from Beth Moore:

*"Remember Christ came to set the captive free. Satan comes to make the free captive. Christ wants to cut some binding ropes from our lives while Satan wants to use them to tie us in knots. Which of the following more nearly fits the original temptation Satan set before our first parents? The answer: eating the fruit will make you strong and independent."*

As I closed my eyes to meditate on these words, once again I saw the carousel.

> I looked up and saw little Katie just crashing from the first crippled horse. There on the revolving floor next to her freshly skinned knee was a shiny red apple. She picked it up, studied it as if it were speaking to her, and then flashed Jesus her look of blame. I watched as the unknowing little girl took one big, juicy bite and carelessly tossed the apple over her shoulder. The poisonous fruit rolled and then settled into the spot on the ground where I had first seen it days before.

As I watched the vision play out, I shuddered as I realized that the serpent had been there. When my horse fell and crashed to the ground, Satan handed me the fruit of disbelief in God. That's why I looked at Jesus with anger and blame when I fell off the horse. The apple, just as it had with Eve, delivered a message from Satan the deceiver: "See what happens when you trust God? You get hurt. You have to be your own boss to secure the life you truly want. God is dangerous; you can only trust yourself."

Satan's first attack against Eve was to trick her into believing that God was withholding something good from her, and that in order to be satisfied, she would have to be in charge. The seed was sown, the seed of disbelief in God's goodness and wisdom. The moment the apple touched Eve's lips, independence took root in her now sinful heart, and dependence on God was removed. The battle for control between spirit and flesh had begun and has descended throughout the generations. Satan led Eve in the ways of distrust by enticing her to believe that God was a stingy liar and didn't know how to take care of her.

As I continued to meditate on the truth imparted to me, I remembered that it was not the first time Jesus had appeared to me on a horse. Instantly, another vision I had during the first months after we lost Anna came to mind.

## THE WHITE HORSE AND THE SWORD

I sat down in the big chair in the corner of the living room, just a few months pregnant with John, hoping to spend some quiet and comforting moments in God's presence. Instead, anger grabbed hold of me. I closed my blurry eyes...

> Jesus was sitting next to me in the chair with His arm around me. Suddenly, a knife was in my hands, and I turned, enraged, to thrust it into His chest. Jesus lovingly and gently took the knife from me and spoke these words, "You are aiming at the wrong person." He pointed, directing me to look ahead. I saw Jesus riding upon a white horse; from His side He pulled a sword, and He reached over and thrust it at Satan, proclaiming, "That was for Anna."

As I contemplated this disturbing and painful vision from my past, I was pierced with shame. I closed my eyes and was once again staring at the carousel. Just as before, Jesus sat on the painted, lifeless horse. But then...

> Jesus turned to me, not the little girl on the carousel, but to me in the present. The horse came to life. Drained of all color and decoration, it leapt as white as snow from the stage of the carousel. Jesus rode toward me, pulling the pole from the center of the horse which had once held Him to the carousel, and I watched as the pole became Christ's sword. And then I knew: His "allow" didn't eradicate or undermine His ultimate victory.

I grew up dreaming of a prince on a white horse, the perfect fairy tale, the perfect ending. Now the book of Revelation revealed that my longing was an imprint, a premonition of a very true reality:

*And I looked and saw there a white horse with a rider holding a bow, given a crown, riding forth as a conqueror bent on conquest...Its rider is called Faithful and True. With justice He judges and makes war...out of His mouth comes a sharp sword... (Revelation 6:2; 19: 11,15)*

As we live, we have a Jesus who rides with us on the carousel of life, comforts us when we fall, and picks us up to put us on new horses. But a day is coming when Jesus the companion will present Himself as Jesus the King, the avenger of life's greatest sorrows, the champion who will ride forth into victory. God's sovereign power, His omnipotence and control, were demonstrated to me through a pole holding a broken horse to a carousel. Though broken, it was still held to the ride by the pole. God's power held it in place. God also showed me that this same pole will one day become a sword. The power used to "hold us" will be the same power used to conquer our enemy. We may not be able to understand how fallen horses (our earthly losses) are within God's loving control, yet we are still "held" by Him. His sovereign power which holds us securely to Him during our earthly life and losses will be the same power which rescues and avenges us. We will be defended for the defenseless moments we endured on earth.

I was beginning to comprehend that God's sovereignty doesn't mean He causes tragedy, making Him cruel. Rather, He is in control in the midst of tragedy, making Him good. I was learning that to trust God in tragedy was to trust that His holiness and perfection held together the broken pieces of my life in such a way that to God, it wasn't broken at all. I was beginning to understand that my resistance to God's sovereignty throughout our loss was due to an agreement I'd made with the deceiver. "If God had withheld from me, He must not be good and therefore trustworthy"... chomp! Just like Eve, I had taken a bite of the fruit.

A couple weeks later I sat in church contemplating the carousel and subsequent visions. The white horse, the rider, the sword, and the message of victory consumed me. Then my mind began reeling through all of the turmoil and pain I knew of in the lives of others. I saw a family suffering with the cancer that had afflicted a young mother. Her adoring husband had his arms around her and their two small children. Suddenly, in the middle of their huddle, I saw a pole.

After church, a woman approached me in tears to share with me that her nephew had just lost their first baby at thirty-eight weeks gestation. I wept with her. She described the grave with a fence built around it at a family farm. As I prayed for them, suddenly, behind the gravestone, I saw a pole.

And then I saw, positioned in pain for my sin, Jesus hanging on the cross. I realized the cross is a pole. Erected high, it speaks of God's control in the midst of our deepest tragedies, the ones that seem beyond help and lost from the grip of God's good, strong hands. It promises power over death, new life, and new hope for those who have kneeled under the showers of forgiveness – the blood of Christ Jesus. I was reminded that Jesus Himself was once controlled by darkness, yet God never lost control. He had a plan. The tomb was empty. Jesus is alive! The cross points to the day when we will look and see Jesus riding forth on a white horse as a conqueror. Jesus Himself took a moment during His humble earthly life to proclaim, *Do not suppose that I have come to bring peace to the earth. I did not come to bring peace, but a sword (Matt 10:34).*

All this said, faith in God in the presence of tragedy is just so hard. Scripture urges us to have the faith of a child. *I tell you the truth, anyone who will not receive the kingdom of God like a little child shall not enter it (Mark 10:15).* Why would we be encouraged to have such a simplistic view of God?

As a little girl, a simple sentence spoken by my mom and dad set my heart at ease and invited my feelings into safety time and time again. Whether in response to a bad dream, hurt feelings, or an even greater fear like death, "It's going to be all right" was a magic sentence. It's not really an answer to anything. I hear myself say it to my children when they're upset as I pull them into my chest and stroke their hair. "There, there now, Mommy's here. Everything's going to be all right." As a child I never once said to my mom, "How? How do you know it's going to be all right?" I simply trusted her and let myself rest within the care and protection of her confidence, power, and authority as my mom. I just believed that she must know something I didn't in order to be able to assert that everything was going to be okay. The combination of her presence, coupled with her knowledge and her role as my parent, the one who was in control and in charge of me, was powerful. This combination is really a parent's expression of the sovereignty of God. All the components are there: the omniscience (knowledge), the omnipresence (presence), and the omnipotence (power).

Looking back, I wish I could have allowed myself to be child in God's arms and to trust His proclamation that *everything was going to be all right.* It's a non-answer kind of answer. It's not a "how" or a "why." It's a non-specific response requiring trust. I was too mature, too intellectual, too untrusting to be able to simply rest within His assurance that "everything was going to be all right." I wanted answers. "When? How? Why?" I demanded! I wanted an explanation. "Why did Anna die? Why did You allow it? Why is there infertility? Why is there cancer? Why are there earthquakes leaving thousands of children orphaned from their crushed parents?" For peace with God in the midst of the mind-boggling difficulties and tragedies of life, I was learning that I must trust with child-like faith. He truly is the only One who can make everything, including the tragic, wrong things, *all* right!

"There, there now, everything is going to be all right… the horse is still on the pole." I am reminded that in my play date with Jesus on the carousel, braids and all, I was a child. When He extended His hand and offered a new horse, I took it. It was a simple response. Yes, I'd been mad and frustrated that He had let me fall, but I quickly got over it and hopped onto the next horse. It was Jesus, after all. Children can do that. They are resilient, they forgive easily, and they trust.

My sovereign God may not give me all the answers I want or feel I need in this lifetime. He may not do away with suffering or send me a letter of explanation in the mail. But what He has offered me is Himself. He is Sovereign, which means I can look forward to the white horse, to the rider who will defend and dismantle the enemy, giving me the ultimate victory I long for. It is my birthright as a child of a sovereign God.

That same morning in church, though I was weeping, I attempted to sing "Our Great God." My heart, penetrated by His love, surrendered to gratitude and service to Jesus, my Sovereign rescuer, in a whole new way. The following lyrics stayed with me all afternoon:

> *Lord we are weak and frail, helpless in the storm.*
> *Surround us with your angels; hold us in your arms.*
> *Our cold and ruthless enemy; his pleasure is our harm.*
> *Rise Up, O Lord, and he will flee before our Sovereign God.*
> *Hallelujah! Glory be to Our Great God!*

I am a mother who has grieved, who has fought with God because I bought into the devil's accusations against Him. With the forbidden fruit in hand, I stood on the wrong side of the battlefield. Today as I write, I find myself weeping over my sin in grief, my blame of a God I assumed was much less than perfect. Now with a right and holy view of God in place, it seems impossible that I offered Him anything more than my tears, love, and need for His saving grace. I am sad that I condemned Him. But it's true; it's a part of my story, and I am forgiven, loved, and redeemed by a sovereign, good God! I cannot even begin to express the longing I have for my victory day, for the moment I am avenged by my loving, all-powerful Savior. But for now, with the faith of a child, I am resting in the knowledge of His sovereignty and the truth that I am held by Him. After all, my horse is still on the pole, and everything is going to all right!

CHAPTER 15

# FAREWELL

*'If you want to give it all you've got,' Jesus replied,*
*'relinquish everything. Then come follow me.' That was*
*the last thing the young man expected to hear. And so,*
*crest-fallen, he walked away. He was holding on tight*
*to a lot of things, and he couldn't bear to let go.*

*Matthew 19:21-22*

"Have you said good-bye to Anna?" was the counselor's question that reduced me to tears. I knew the answer, though I had fought and reasoned against the final adieu I had tried so hard to avoid. Was it necessary? She had been dead for nearly four years. I knew she was gone. I'd let go of more and more of her throughout the years as I said yes to more and more earthly responsibility. Releasing Anna's spirit seemed to be the last and final step toward healing and the crucial element of accepting her death and taking the reins of my life at hand. I had to let her go. So many visions had hinted to that reality. I had worked so hard to understand the spiritual realm we live in and had received such insight about heaven. I feared that letting go of Anna would diminish the tremendous love I had for her, or that I would have to stop thinking about her and her heavenly life. I just didn't want to let go.

The evening before counseling, as I was watching television, I had been impaled by grief over a heart-wrenching scene of letting go. An elderly man stood pumping his wife's chest for hours trying to keep her alive even though he knew it was hopeless and had previously agreed to an order of "do not resuscitate." Finally another doctor came, took over the rhythmic gesture toward life, and then gently let go so the man wouldn't have to be the one to do it. I curled up on my bed at the end of the scene and wept bitterly, recalling the day of Anna's birth and my own memory of being forced to let go of her body. Now, four years later, my task would be letting go of her spirit. I just didn't want to do it. I had worked so hard to hang onto her that letting go of her seemed unbearably final. I was afraid of what it would cost me. As I sat there with my counselor, tears streaming down my face, I suddenly remembered my first lesson in life and loss.

When I was six years old, I had found a turtle in the woods near our house. I brought it home and pretended she was my little green-shelled baby for a couple of days. The turtle started to look ill, and at my mother's instruction, I was to take her back to the woods to release her. I remember taking her out of the box, setting her down on the ground, and turning to come home. Two steps, and I simply couldn't abandon her. I scooped her back up and ran blubbering all the way home and into the house. "Mama, I can't do it. I can't let her go. I can't leave her there." My mom, understanding the enormity of this loss in the context of my innocence, knelt beside me and said, "Katie, the little turtle needs to go find her mommy. If you don't let her go, she will never find her. If you love her, you will let her go."

It was the exact speech I needed to be able to make the trek back to the woods to set her down. I wanted her to have the best life possible, which I now knew meant she would be with her mama. I remember my heart aching as I walked away empty-handed.

This vivid memory reminded me that love lets go in order for the one you love to be released to the best life possible. I needed to encourage Anna to run to Jesus. Like a mama bird nudging her baby out of the nest, I needed to say farewell.

Just a few months after we lost Anna, my prayer one evening had been interrupted by a strange vision:

> A little girl adorned with braids sat with her hands cupping her face, her elbows resting on her knees. She was obviously sad and sat with her head bent down, sitting on a flight of stairs. I knew it was Anna, and I heard myself ask her, "What's wrong, sweetie?" She looked up and replied, "I just miss you guys."

You would think I would have been touched by the image of my daughter longing for us. But it had disturbed me greatly. It hadn't seemed right that Anna, sealed in heaven, surrounded by angels, and in the presence of Jesus, *could* be sad. Additionally, it had bothered me because the visions I'd had thus far were entirely upheld and consistent with Scripture. How could Anna be sad in the presence of God? It just didn't make sense, until Jesus finally revealed its significance and meaning within the final step of letting her go.

Now, after a long and painfully thoughtful silence, I answered the counselor's looming question. "No, I have not said good-bye to Anna." I explained that I was afraid letting her go would mean letting go of the enormous love I had for her. So we simply asked Jesus what letting go would mean.

> I saw Mary, the mother of Jesus, cradling her son just hours after His birth. As she laid Him down for His first night in the manger, she lifted her hands, and from her grasp flew a dove.

His spirit never *belonged* to her. From the moment of Jesus' birth, Mary was called to release Him back to her heavenly Father. After I saw this image, I sensed these words from the Lord: "I will only ever take that which isn't true." My love for Anna wasn't a lie, so I knew good-bye couldn't take it away. I wondered if somehow releasing her would in fact strengthen my love for her.

The counselor prayed, "Jesus, show Kate...does she need to release Anna's spirit? Does she need to say good-bye?" I sat blankly for a moment, and then he prayed, "Lord I feel led to ask what Anna wants. What does Anna want her mother to do?" At that, I began weeping, and I saw a set of images, like home video clips, play out before me.

Chris and I stood joyfully before Jesus, who held infant Anna in an open field of grass. It was a familiar scene, one I had received in the very beginning. There was such pleasure in this intimate, complete moment, but I knew I was supposed to walk away. As I started to go, I turned anxiously around, and in desperation I pleaded, "Just one kiss?" Jesus didn't forbid me, but I knew it would make walking away nearly impossible. So once again, I turned and started to walk away. After a moment, I glanced back over my shoulder to see Jesus with the little bundle of Anna cradled in His arms, walking back toward the horizon whence He had come.

As I turned back around, I saw, just as in my vision years before, a very sad Anna sitting at the bottom of the stairs, and without hesitation, I began to run toward her, shouting as if at a football game, "Go, Go, Go!" She stood and turned giddy with delight. I hit her bottom as she raced up each step, continually chanting, "Go, Go, Go"! When she reached the top of the steps, she opened a gate and ran into the very field we had just been in together. She ran without looking back into the distance to catch up with Jesus. Again I saw mother Mary, arms lifted, hands extended, releasing the spirit of baby Jesus into the heavens. I nearly heard the voice of Jesus whispering to the furthest corners of my soul, *Do not hinder them, for the kingdom of heaven belongs to such as these (Matthew 13:14).*

I finally understood why Jesus had opened my eyes to the vision of Anna missing us. He sought to reveal to me that Anna would not want her parents to be so miserable in her absence. She was sad for her mother and father. She missed the "us" she had known during her nine months of life, but we had since become nearly unrecognizable to her. All the truths I had prayed for Anna to know, I was barely clinging to myself. I am not a Biblical scholar, nor am I an expert in the spiritual realm. But one thing I do know is that *Jesus can do exceedingly abundantly more than all we ask or imagine (Ephesians 3:20).* If God wanted Anna to see us or pray for us in our spiritual battle, God could make it happen. I imagine that if God were to permit such a viewing, Anna would definitely feel a burden of sadness for the dismal life her parents were living. Whether Anna actually was sad for us or not, I do not know. But God used this vision of Anna to speak to my reluctant heart. God wanted me to say good-bye and to move on with my life. I was doing Anna no favors by hanging on.

My dad always smacked our bottoms as we raced up the stairs to bed each night, a playful gesture at hurrying us along.

I love the thought of hurrying Anna into her eternal destiny, freeing her to live within the life we were all created for. Not that Anna needed it, but I was giving her my blessing to go and be full in her life in Christ. I think I needed it. I needed to know that I was able to encourage her to run into eternity, the life she was always designed and intended for. As I turned away from the steps of the vision, I saw before me my life, my husband, and my sons. Releasing Anna allowed me to fully embrace the relationships God had for me to nurture in this life. I was coming home a better wife and a better mother. If Anna had truly witnessed my final farewell from the balconies of heaven, then she would know there was no need to miss me anymore. In letting go, I received a new way to live in freedom.

On my way home from counseling, I stopped by the store to pick up a few last minute ingredients for supper. As I walked in the door, I saw the most beautiful bouquet of pink roses. I bought the whole bundle and determined right there that the rest of the day would be a celebration day. Saying good-bye had welcomed Anna and me into a whole new way of living. This was a definite cause for celebration, and I imagined that such a gala was taking place in heaven as well.

That evening as I rocked baby Ben to sleep, I pondered the tremendous step I had taken in releasing Anna. I had surrendered her, finally, into the good hands of God and made it known to her that mama was okay. In fact, mama was soaring. I relived the vision from earlier that day and gathered the courage to say out-loud the good-bye that had silently taken place in my spirit. I wanted to become comfortable with the notion of having released her. With my eyes tightly shut and my heart fully open, I said over and over, growing in confidence and making sure not to take it back: "Good-bye, Good-bye,

Good-bye." When I opened my eyes and beheld sweet baby Ben, sleeping in the crook of my arms, I couldn't help but say, "Hello, Hello, Hello." It was like I was seeing him for the first time. I was truly ready to live.

The next morning God impressed upon my heart that this very lesson in releasing the dead we love so dearly was already established in His Word. The following is an account of Mary Magdalene and her first encounter with her beloved Jesus after His resurrection.

*She turned to leave the empty tomb and saw someone standing there. It was Jesus, but she didn't recognize Him. 'Dear woman, why are you crying?' Jesus asked her. 'Who are you looking for?' She thought He was the gardener. 'Sir,' she said, 'if you have taken Him away, tell me where you have put Him, and I will go and get Him.' 'Mary!' Jesus said. She turned to Him and cried out, 'Rabboni' (teacher). 'Don't cling to me,' Jesus said, 'for I haven't yet ascended to the Father. But go find my brothers and tell them, I am ascending to My Father and your Father, to My God and your God' (John 20: 14-17).*

As I read these timeless words from John's gospel, I sensed they were now being written on the tablet of my heart. I identified so much with Mary's desire to take care of and nurture the beloved dead. From the sound of her name rolling off His tongue, she recognized that the man before her was in fact the dead, but risen Jesus for whom she had felt such love and responsibility. She must have lunged for Him, buried her head in His chest, and locked her arms around His waist as if to say, "I am never letting go." Can you imagine for a moment how you would respond if the deceased person you hold so dear appeared before you right now? I imagine that Jesus, knowing every longing in Mary's heart and her desire for Him, spoke tenderly yet firmly, "Mary do not cling to Me; I am headed for heaven. Don't get too comfortable with Me, Mary; don't hold on too tightly, for I am just passing through." Now I could hear Jesus saying to me, tenderly yet firmly, "My dear Katie, do not cling to Anna any longer. Let her go, and let her come to Me. Do not be afraid; I am your Redeemer."

These lessons in life, of loss and letting go, bring to mind the precious and sacred words of musician and songwriter Chris Rice's "Untitled Hymn." I will adopt his words as my own...

*And with your final heartbeat*
*kiss the world goodbye.*
*Then go in peace, and laugh on Glory's side, and*
*fly to Jesus*
*fly to Jesus*
*fly to Jesus and live!*[10]

The day Anna Rose Katherine Kelty died was the day I died. My rebirth in Christ has ushered me into the resurrection of those who have met the Jesus of the wounded, the weak and the broken...the Savior of the sad. There is one final thing to say to the sweet baby girl who bears my mark in eternity: *thank you.* Your precious life has saved mine. One day, Anna, we'll get it all back. Death can't keep anything from us that heaven isn't bursting to renew. Until then, play and worship at the feet of Jesus. Before too long, you'll see me coming across the horizon in that great lush field we've already shared. And when you see me coming...run!

---

[10] Rice, Chris "Untitled Hymn (Come to Jesus)" <u>Run the Earth, Watch the Sky</u> 2003.

PART FIVE

# PEACE

# Living

*To live is Christ – to die is gain.*
*Life versus more life – I can't lose.*

*Phil 1:21 (NIV, MSG)*

Many years have passed since I said my farewell to Anna and my hello to life. I have grieved with Jesus and not against Him. There is peace along with the sadness. There is joy amidst the pain of her absence. But she *is* absent and there *is* sorrow.

I had hoped the years would take it away. I had hoped that just as time delivered good gifts to us, it would also deliver freedom from grief. But it is still here, the ache and sadness that exist because she does not. Each anniversary brings grief, and every year it rages and rips through to the very core of who I am. I have stopped expecting it to be any different. Instead, I allow the anticipation for the moments Jesus will come and rescue me to grow alongside the grief. Year seven taught me this. Year seven taught me to stop bracing myself and to press into the pain, to press into the heart of the One who always rescues me in the dark. And for this I am grateful. Grief has made me rich. Grief has given, and always will give, me Jesus.

This book begins with a graveyard, five years before grief became my reality. I was led there by the Spirit into a place of death to discover a secret nook of glory, of beauty, of Eden. Years have passed, but I have since discovered that this little nook was a preemptive and sovereign gift – a glimpse at the secret place God would create within my own soul to rescue me every day, every moment in the graveyard of my grief. This is a place where Shepherd rescues sheep, where night gives birth to day, and sorrow awakens the spirit to His good, redeeming, and constant presence. This is the place I write from today. It is the place from which I pray I continue to live my life – the beautiful heart of a God who will always be enough for me.

As I bring this story to a close, I offer this epilogue, a few final glimpses of the Jesus of my grief.

## ANNA'S SEVENTH BIRTHDAY

The boys were absolutely giddy when I came home with them...my face lost in the pink mass as I made my way through the front door. The smiles that accompany their Anna joy dig deep into my heart, deep to the Anna spot.

We each grabbed a few strings and made our way into the yard, February air quickening us to the task that always greets me with a smile and a sting. This year, ten-month-old baby Elijah hugged my hip. It was his first year to behold our annual balloon show. Chris counted to three, we declared a collective "We love you Anna," and then as the strings slipped from clutched fingers, once again, I let go. Once again I felt the joy and pain that always comes with Anna.

*Watching Anna's Birthday Balloons*

We watched the balloons soaring high, searching for heaven's door. We watched them until we could not see them any longer. We imagined Anna waiting with eager anticipation, our giggling girl thrust back by a love attack from her family. I stared at the sky, staring at what could not be seen, and I felt sick with sadness. The boys raced toward the door petitioning me to come serve the cupcakes and ice-cream. I reluctantly turned away from *her* home to ours, a shift I have made a thousand times before, and I ducked away for a moment to feel the pain. Chris gave me the look, the one that says, "We're in this together," and I chose the joy part and not the pain part for that particular moment. I conjured up my best mama smile and said, "Who likes cupcakes?"

I clutched baby Elijah extra tight as I carried Him up the stairs for bed that night. The older boys played games downstairs with their daddy, so I took off my smile and replaced it with the sadness I really felt. I was quickly melting into a puddle of pain and desperation. I looked deep into the baby, hoping that his calm, sleepy presence, his helpless trust, would invite me to the same. I hoped that I could get lost in joy just by looking at him. But all I could see in that moment was the nothingness of Anna.

I turned off the light in the nursery and made my way to our sacred nook in the corner of the room. I sat down in the rocking chair, the one that has allowed me to rock four babies, the one that has rocked me too. I was overcome, nursing one, grieving another. I closed my eyes, seeking to silence the sobs, trying to hush the heaving and not wanting to wake the baby. I shut my eyes, seeking to suppress the pain I hate to feel. But as I shut down, the eyes of my heart were opened.

I found myself staring at the back of a little girl, her long hair sweeping down over a white linen dress. She bent over, reaching down, scooping something. As she turned around to greet me, her hand extended, and she offered me a cup. I saw clearly that the girl, *my* girl, was standing in front of a well. I took the cup from her and drank a sip of what turned out to be something of deep satisfaction and peace – a sip that revived me. As I looked up from the cup and back to Anna, I discovered she was sitting on the wall of the well and around her small, pretty frame was the arm of Jesus. The whispered phrase *Living Water* arrived like a welcomed guest beckoning entrance into the home of my heart. I stared at the two of them, Jesus and the daughter we share, cozy and nestled against one other. I stared at them, and they stared back at me, the space in between filled with expectation, peace, and joy.

I opened my eyes to behold the sweet sleeping boy in my arms. My grief was supernaturally turned to peace lined with curiosity. I stared at him and pondered *living water*. I closed my eyes again to reflect, and in a flash the sparkling eyes and joyful face of Jesus were just inches away. I braced myself, and for a few moments, not a single breath escaped. The image was more vivid and alive than the vision of moments before, so real it seemed a flash of reality, a glimpse at something... do I dare say it was actually there? I was alive with a sense of wonder at this holy moment, and then I heard it again, *living water*.

I paused briefly, and then I stood slowly and walked to the crib, gently placing the baby down to a night of rest. *Rest*, I felt it now too. The sip of living water had given me that.

I stood in the hallway outside the nursery for a frozen moment. A flame had just been lit in the darkness of my grief, a flame called "the Way the Truth and the Life" (John 14:6). I had just been given a candle to light the way through this corridor of pain, the path I knew would continue on until eternity.

## LIVING WATER

That evening I fell asleep peacefully, worn out by grief, but comforted deeply and thoroughly by my encounter with Jesus and Anna. Living Water had rescued me, and I was determined to understand every beautiful part of the miracle. I knew God's word held the answers, and I knew He was leading me to the woman at the well.

I read the account from John, chapter four over and over again. Having just seen it all so clearly in my vision, it was easy to jump into the pages of scripture. I could nearly feel the dusty earth of Samaria under my feet, the heat of the noon sun parching my tongue to match the yearning of my heart. And I very quickly discovered our likeness...our thirst.

Perhaps she had wept sorrow's tears before coming to the well. Jesus identifies her as one who'd had five husbands, and the man she presently was with was not a husband at all. I can only imagine the layers of pain, her life losses. Was she a widow, divorced? Was she a prostitute? What dark threads of grief, pain, and shame laced her years? I imagine her sad story called out to Jesus long before He reached Samaria, alluring Him to come. He sat on the wall of the well, and He waited for her. Thirsty she came, and with compassion and promise He spoke, "*Whoever drinks the water I give them will never thirst. Indeed, the water I give them will become in them a spring of water welling up to eternal life*" (John 4:13-14.)

Her pain was a symptom of her thirst, her ultimate longing for Jesus. God sought to reveal the same to me. My grief was ultimately a symptom of my longing for the remedy, the Living Water, the satiating solution of God.

Just a couple of chapters later, recorded in the book of John, Jesus talks about the Living Water again,

*On the last and greatest day of the festival, Jesus stood and said in a loud voice, "Let anyone who is thirsty come to me and drink. Whoever believes in me, as Scripture has said, rivers of living water will flow from within them." By this he meant the Spirit, whom those who believed in Him were later to receive. Up to that time the Spirit had not been given, since Jesus had not yet been glorified."( John 7: 37-38 )*

On the Eve of Anna's seventh Birthday, I was gifted a miracle. In my grief, my eyes were opened to the reality of the Living Water, to the beauty of the indwelling spirit of God. I had met Jesus in my grief over and over again, but in this particular grief-saturated moment, I had given up. I had surrendered to grief and allowed it to Lord over me, and then the vision came. God pierced the darkness and awakened my collapsing spirit to a cup, a girl, a God. It was powerful, and I was rescued, and I determined that never again would I grieve without the Living Water.

It was Anna who extended the cup, asking me to look not upon her, but upon the answer her tiny, precious hand beheld. She was urging me to shift my focus, from her to Him, from death to life. It was as if she pleaded, "*Here mama, living water, drink.*" Just like a caretaker pushing fluids to nurse a sick patient back to health, she knew I needed Jesus. She knew my grief was desperately crying out to be quenched by the presence and provision of God. In my pain, I had forgotten to reach for the cup. I was refusing to be comforted, refusing to see what was before me. But once again, Anna gave me Jesus. She gave me the Living Water, and she introduced me to a holy and satisfying way to grieve.

As I write today, two more years have passed, nearly a decade of loving and longing for my girl. I deeply love my three little boys and am presently expecting our fourth son. I am captivated by their lives and count the blessings I have been entrusted with daily, yet deep in my heart there is a wound which I know cannot be healed until heaven offers me redemption. But I am drinking the Living Water, and I do experience miraculous measures of comfort, strength, and joy in the midst of continued grief.

The answer in every moment of my life, every exhausted, worn-out, thirsty moment, will always be Jesus, and it is effortless to get to Him. Coming home to Jesus is never a journey that takes more than an instant, because the well that holds the Living Water is within. I won't ever be able to get rid of the pain, but I can in every moment of my grief dip into myself, into the well of my soul, and retrieve the God who comforts, strengthens, sustains, and births joy from the dark canal of grief. This story has taught me over and over that my pursuit of God has always been more about His pursuit of me. God longs to satisfy His wounded, thirsty children with Himself.

There are two little words that linger in the air of Calvary that I have always read over so quickly. But after being acquainted with my thirst and my need for the Living Water, these words grip me now. From the cross Jesus cried out,

*I thirst.* (John 19:38)

For the first time in His life, Jesus' soul was disconnected from the source of satisfaction, and He was parched by sin, grief, and pain. Jesus was thirsty. He longed to be reconnected to the source of satisfaction, to be quenched by the God who had turned His face away. It was this moment when Jesus took the full measure of the venom of sin upon Himself, and in conquering death, He became the anecdote. He became the Living Water, the remedy for every disconnected, thirsty heart.

I still have a thousand questions that begin and end with why, but those questions have lost their need to be answered underneath the revelation of the one answer I do have. Jesus died and conquered death for me, and therefore, resurrection is a reality for me as well. Measures of redemption have been planned for me this side of heaven, and full redemption is waiting for me in eternity. My thirst can be quenched. All I have to do is live in the awareness of His presence, continually yielding and surrendering my life, my pain, and my plans to Him, trusting that He is enough for me.

In the sad moments of my life, I reach for the cup, I sip, and there is comfort for sorrow. In the moments of loneliness, I sip, and there is a supernatural presence to hold me. In the moments when I am lost in confusion and uncertainty, I sip, and there is truth and promise to sustain and uphold. In moments of fear, I sip, and the name of Jesus conquers the enemy, thief of truth and peace. And in the moments when the burden of grief is so great that no earthly joy can repair it, I sip, and the burden-bearer lifts mourning and touches my wounds with peace.

There is a jewel tucked away in the psalms that I have now adopted as my life's soul-song. It will accompany me on the rest of this journey. It speaks of thirst, proclaims the Living Water, and portrays a soul-satisfied response:

*"You, God, are my God, earnestly I seek you; I thirst for you, my whole being longs for you, in a dry and parched land where there is no water. I have seen you in the sanctuary and beheld your power and your glory. Because your love is better than life, my lips will glorify you. I will praise you as long as I live, and in your name I will lift up my hands. I will be fully satisfied as with the richest of foods and with singing lips I will praise You"* (Psalm 63: 1).

Pain, provision, and praise: these few verses take a thirsty soul, they offer it *love better than life,* and then the satisfied soul begins to sing. This soul begins to praise. This satiated life is now a *child of worship*...and now my story has come full circle.

## CHILD OF WORSHIP

That's what I heard nearly ten years ago when I asked Jesus, "What shall I pray for the baby?" and *Child of worship* rose like a sweet vapor from the indwelling Spirit to my mind. As I sat down to write these final words, I petitioned, "Jesus, show me how it all ends?" As bright and clear as day, I heard it again... *Child of worship.*

Jesus Christ is calling *me* to be a child of worship. He always was. The prayer, though offered for Anna, has always been God's greatest desire for me. He knew that if I made my home within this phrase, that I would nestle into the little valley in the center of the cemetery, the peace, joy, and satisfaction that exist in the experience of adoring God.

I used to think worship was a song, or designated moments spent praising God. But I have come to learn that worship is much more than that. Worship is a way of thinking and being; it is a way to live. It is the truest form of a purposeful life, for worshipping God is what we were designed to do. Growing in grief by grace has completely redefined my experience and perspective of worship, and it is simply this: everything that I am, surrendered, to receive and reflect everything that He is. My life, every moment I exist, is to be a compliment to God. I am to be a round of applause to His wonderful love and perfection. I have learned, and am continuing to learn, that as I trade my worship of all else for worship of Jesus alone, I am becoming who I have always longed to be.

For me, being a child of worship means staring into the face of Jesus on the bitter days as well as on the best days, while loving Him and absorbing His love for me. Being a child of worship is kneeling at His feet and knowing that the truest fulfillment and satisfaction I will ever feel is to know Him. It is within the child of worship experience that I can utter the phrase, *I consider everything a loss compared to the surpassing greatness of knowing Christ Jesus my Lord, for whose sake I have lost all things. I consider them rubbish that I may gain Christ and be found in Him (Philippians 3:8).* Being a child of worship means accepting my life with all of its light and dark sentences and thanking God for what He has given me to trust him and glorify Him with. In worship, I claim His presence as all I will ever need.

Worshipping and praising God by naming His attributes is the quickest way to drink the Living Water. It opens the floodgates and unleashes the power it contains to resurrect the dead places within. In worship, lies bow down to truth, pain makes room for peace, and grief surrenders to joy. In worship, I crawl grieving and poor to the foot of the cross and walk away rich in the love, grace and provision of Jesus.

Child of worship is how this story began, and child of worship is how it will end. My testimony is now complete.

## REDEMPTION

I suppose the last word I shall record here is the one I find myself repeating most often these days. It is the word that ushers me from moments of pain into moments of peace. It is the word leading me on from darkness to the ultimate of mornings. It is a small word, a word possessing great power, a word that thrives in the living water.

Hope.

It is tucked into verse after verse of the beautiful book my grief has led me to cherish. The place in which I have found it to be the most sacred and precious is in this exhortation from Paul:

*May the God of hope fill you with all joy and peace as you trust and believe in Him and that your hearts may overflow with hope by the power of the Holy Spirit (Romans 15:13).*

It was Chris who first presented this scripture to me for a painting to hang in Anna's nursery. He searched for weeks until he found this verse and just knew it was the right one for his girl. In the early years of grief and fighting, my mind and heart could not be blessed by it. Now of course, it means everything. I can see now, as I look back into Anna's empty nursery, this scripture hanging over the empty crib, the kindness and sweetness of God in urging Chris to choose this verse above all others. It was never for Anna. It was always His promise for us. "Believe in me, Kate and Chris, as you weep in this place of pain. Trust in me, your God of hope, and I will fill you with all peace and joy, and I will overflow your hearts with hope." How very true these words have become in our lives.

It was during an afternoon nap with John a few years ago when *hope* came to life for me. I have been transformed by it ever since.

Long, silvery-gray hair glistened. All I could see were the shiny, coarse strands until the panoramic view widened, and an old woman rocked on a front porch in bright afternoon sun. Her hair draped over her right shoulder, and her eyes stared deep into the distance. A book was pressed open against her chest. As if she were taking a break from reading, one full breath caused her to close her eyes. I watched and waited only to gasp a breath myself, when I realized that this intriguing stranger would not be opening her eyes again. She was dead. Quite suddenly the scene shifted, and now I saw a young woman crouching down in a field of tall grass, arms extended. At breakneck speed a few yards away, a little girl sprinted, book in hand, jumping into the woman's arms. At that very moment, I began to see the vision from the inside out. I was no longer viewing the scene from above, but from the very eyes of the woman who embraced the little girl. In the distance, Jesus approached with a knowing look of joy, and then I realized, it was *me*, the old woman who had died.

On February 25, 2005, I held a beautiful, lifeless, baby girl in my arms. Every day since, I have remembered this pain. Every day since, I have been held myself. The One who holds me is strong. The One who holds me is perfect love. The One who holds me is worthy of my trust and deserving of my worship.

One day not too far from now, my eyes will close, and in heaven they will open. I will see my Savior approaching, and I will hear Him say, "Come to the living water, Kate, and never thirst again." I will run to Him, and I will finally embrace the One who held me all those years in the dark. He will hold up His nail-scarred hands to my face, and the last tears I will ever shed will be wiped from my eyes (Isaiah 25:8). In the distance, I will see her running, this book clutched in her hand, and I will crouch down, bracing myself for the hug I will have dreamed of all my life.

But for now...I will satisfy my thirst with love better than life, and I will worship the One who saves me still.

His name is Jesus.

He is the Jesus of my grief.

He is the Jesus of my life.

# Acknowledgements

I am grateful for the opportunity to express thanks to the very dear people God has used to bring comfort and encouragement to me, through grief, healing and the birth of this book.

To my dear parents- from the very beginning, you have blessed me with your grief, grace and faithfulness. You comforted and encouraged me when suffering nearly consumed me. Thank you for the gift of your love and faith. To David, thank you for a lifetime of tenderness and for caring for Anna and me in such a gentle way, then and now. Thank you for giving me a record of her life I will forever cherish. And Kristen, you have endured long and I know you will continue to. Thank you for being the first one to enter the pain and for continuing to climb down into the pit of despair, for whispering the truth to me again and again and for directing me to look up into the eyes of Jesus.

Thank you to my second family, the Kelty's, for opening your hearts to love and support us in our shared pain. To my sweet mother and father-in-law, our hearts are unfortunately now bound by the loss of children. They are also bound by the hope of what Jesus alone can offer us in our suffering. I am so thankful we have each other to grieve and hope with.

To my dearest friends, Montica, Laura and Raegan...your faithfulness and grace revived me in the earliest years of grief and continues to. Where would I be without you? Raegi- I ache for your pain. I long for the day we are laughing with Theo and Anna in heaven. What a day of rejoicing that will be! And to Nicole, Karla, Cait, Erin, Kristin and Ruthy, thank you for feeling and responding to the weight of my grief from the very beginning and for your faithfulness still.

To my girls, Jessica, Rachel, Carrie, and Jill, you were the beautiful gifts God had waiting for me to open when we moved so soon after our loss. Thank you for carrying the corners of the blanket for me. And thank you to Jess and Dee, for seeing for me, hearing for me and for believing and battling for me. To Melissa, you are so much more than just a gift to my brother- you are truly my sister and I am so thankful for the ways you have entered into our story and for how you have been God's grace in my grief. And to Alicia, for "getting it" in a way that few others have- thank you for loving me in and through every season of grief and for longing for our heavenly children together. You are a gift of grief I will forever cherish.

Thank you to my dear church family and friends at Aletheia for your prayers, support and encouragement in grief and in ministry. I love you!

Thank you, Carmen Fowler LaBerge, for being the first professional voice of encouragement and for your continued support in this journey. Thank you, Ruth Graham, for blessing me with your words of confidence and encouragement and for your beautiful endorsement of this book.

Thank you, Stephen Johnson, for inviting me to join you on the healing prayer journey that has forever changed my life and for teaching me that Jesus was and is the healer of all my pain and my sole reason for hope. Thank you, Jim Glanzer, for continuing the healing journey with me and for bringing me to the feet of Jesus, where truth was waiting to restore my heart.

Thank you, Tracy Sonafelt, for your wisdom and beautiful edits. I am so glad you were the one to tie up all the loose ends, bringing this project to completion.

Thank you to my dear friend, Lou McCoy and a very special group of ladies from First Presbyterian Church in Harrisonburg,

Virginia. Thank you to the Bland and Benz families and thank you to our dearest friends, Elton and Montica, you gave this book wings. Thank you for investing in its publication.

And Chris, I can barely type for the tears welling up in my eyes. From the moment we learned we had lost our sweet baby, you have been grace, love, gentleness, patience, tenderness and comfort to me. Thank you for allowing me the time and space to write, but for also encouraging me to do so and for echoing the voice of truth again and again when I have battled the worst lies and fears. You are my greatest earthly treasure and I still pinch myself that I get to be your wife and that we get to raise children together. Thank you for reflecting the true Jesus to me and for making me want to be more like Him.

And lastly to my sweet Anna, you gave me Jesus. Is there anything I could possibly be more thankful for?

# BIBLE TRANSLATIONS

# Note to the Reader

Dear friend in grief,

I am aching with you and for you. I long for you to know peace, to know truth and freedom and to experience abundant measures of comfort, joy and hope. Each journey of grief is unique. Each journey is its own. But the One who holds us and restores us in the dark, *He* is the same. My prayer for you and for myself as we move forward in life with the reality of sorrow is this-

"That from His glorious, unlimited resources He will empower us with inner strength through His Spirit and that Christ will make His home in our hearts as we trust in him. I pray our roots will grow deep into God's love and keep us strong and that may we have the power to understand, how wide, how long, how high, and how deep His love is. I pray that we may experience the love of Christ, though it is too great to understand fully and that we will be made complete with all the fullness of life and power that comes from Him." Ephesians 3:16-19 (NLT)

I would love to know your story and I invite you to reach out to me if you so desire. All my love and hope to you as you journey toward and with the Jesus of your grief,

Kate,
www.TheGraceToGrieve.com
katekelty@gmail.com